MARVEL STUDIOS
VISUAL DICTIONARY

Red hair has
been disguised

Composite
combat armor

Widow's Bite
gauntlet

Electroshock
baton

Holstered
sidearm

Utilitarian
boots

BLACK WIDOW

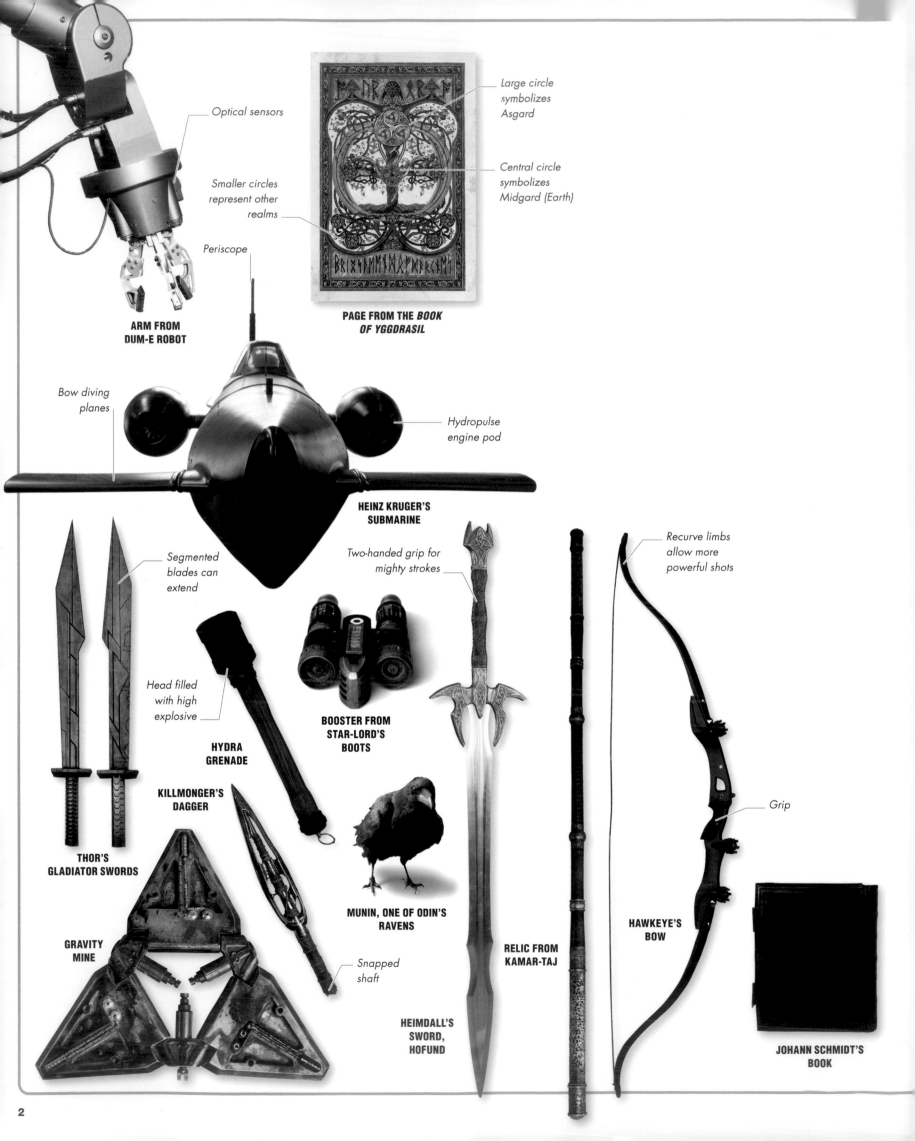

Optical sensors

**ARM FROM
DUM-E ROBOT**

Smaller circles
represent other
realms

Large circle
symbolizes
Asgard

Central circle
symbolizes
Midgard (Earth)

**PAGE FROM THE *BOOK
OF YGGDRASIL***

Periscope

Bow diving
planes

Hydropulse
engine pod

**HEINZ KRUGER'S
SUBMARINE**

Segmented
blades can
extend

Two-handed grip for
mighty strokes

Recurve limbs
allow more
powerful shots

Head filled
with high
explosive

**BOOSTER FROM
STAR-LORD'S
BOOTS**

**HYDRA
GRENADE**

**KILLMONGER'S
DAGGER**

Grip

**THOR'S
GLADIATOR SWORDS**

**GRAVITY
MINE**

**MUNIN, ONE OF ODIN'S
RAVENS**

Snapped
shaft

**RELIC FROM
KAMAR-TAJ**

**HAWKEYE'S
BOW**

**HEIMDALL'S
SWORD,
HOFUND**

**JOHANN SCHMIDT'S
BOOK**

MARVEL STUDIOS
VISUAL DICTIONARY

WRITTEN BY ADAM BRAY

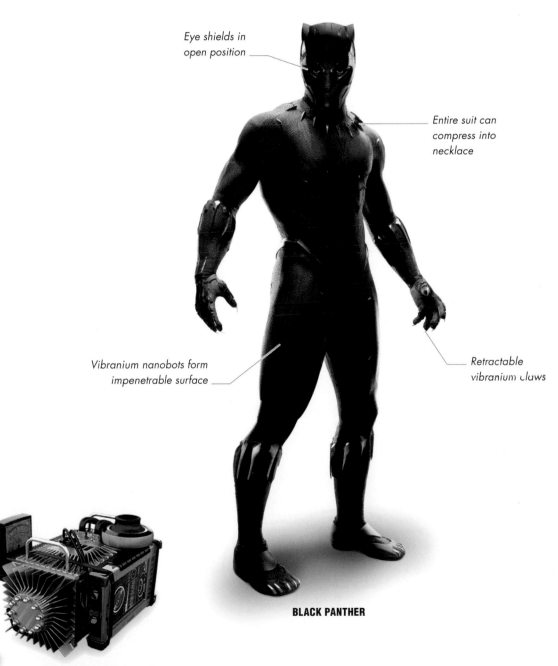

Eye shields in open position

Entire suit can compress into necklace

Vibranium nanobots form impenetrable surface

Retractable vibranium claws

BLACK PANTHER

STAR-LORD'S LOCK PICK

ERIK SELVIG'S PHASE METER

CONTENTS

FOREWORD

I love challenges. When people ask me why I make Super Hero films I always say: "There is a hero in all of us, you just have to dig deep and find the strength." That's what I love about making movies at Marvel Studios. Our characters find the strength in themselves (or in the team) to carry out the task at hand. And so do the cast and crews that make the films all over the world.

I love the challenge of those hurdles. I love to use every technology available to make us more efficient. To be able to tell stories in creative ways you otherwise couldn't. That's the beauty of storytelling through visual effects and sound.

Before I joined *Iron Man*, I had been traveling the world for movie work for about eight years. I'd been away for such a long time and I just wanted to be home in Los Angeles. I joined my friend Louis D'Esposito on a film that went into turnaround for creative reasons (the studio decided not to develop its production any further), and Lou was going on to do another film and asked me to join. "Don't you want to know what it is?" he asked me. I told him I didn't care. As long as it was shooting in LA, I was in. That movie was *Iron Man*.

Before we were finished with *Iron Man*, Kevin Feige offered Lou and me to join what was to become the future home of the Marvel Cinematic Universe. Kevin wanted the three of us to keep making films at what would become Marvel Studios. I told him I would be willing to join if I could be in charge of both visual effects and all of the post-production processes. That way, the potential conflict between editorial and visual effects had to disappear in order for these movies to efficiently work and tell the best stories possible. We had to unite and have one voice leading and constantly protecting only what was best for the movie, not someone's personal agenda.

This foreword serves as my answer to that invitation. It's over ten years later and we've been fortunate enough to introduce the world to an ever-growing, interconnected library of heroes. The complexity and sheer luck of it all doesn't really sink in until you sift through a book such as this. The images in this *Marvel Studios Visual Dictionary* stand as a reminder of every single creative decision that had to be made in order to make a film's release date, yes, but more important, that had to be made in keeping with what would be best for the *characters*.

"Who do you think you work for?"
It's one of the things I always say when I interview people who come to work for us. Of course, they're nervous and the natural response is usually, "Uh…you?"
Nope.
"Marvel Studios?"
Nuh-uh.
And I tell them the answer, in no uncertain terms: "You work for Iron Man. You work for Captain Marvel. You work for the Guardians. You work for Black Panther. Thor. Captain America. Doctor Strange. That's your boss. The boss is the franchise."

After all, we've seen generation after generation of people that have been inspired by our Marvel characters. That's the legacy—and it's one that's never lost on us—when we're working on the films. And I think it's all because of the human spirit. That's the only thing that's going to carry us through.

Every kid deserves to see themselves in our films, regardless of what they look like, regardless of where they come from, regardless of the language they speak, or their religion, or anything at all. They should all be able to have the power to imagine that they can be a Super Hero, that they can save the world. We hope we can ignite that dream in them. ALL of them.

Anyway, I gotta go. The "boss" is calling.

**VICTORIA ALONSO, Executive Vice President
of Physical Production, Marvel Studios**

PREFACIO

Me encantan los desafíos. Cuando la gente me pregunta por qué hago películas de superhéroes, siempre digo: "hay un héroe en todos nosotros, solo toca cavar hasta el fondo de uno mismo y encontrar la fuerza". Por eso me encanta hacer películas en Marvel Studios. Nuestros personajes encuentran la fuerza en sí mismos (o en el equipo) para llevar a cabo la tarea propuesta. Y también lo hacen los elencos y equipos de producción que hacen las películas alrededor del mundo.

Amo el desafío de esos obstáculos. Me encanta usar toda la tecnología disponible para hacernos más eficientes. Para poder contar historias de maneras creativas que de otra manera no podríamos. Esa es la belleza de narrar un cuento a través de los efectos visuales y el sonido.

Antes de volverme parte de IRON MAN, había estado viajando por todo el mundo trabajando en películas durante aproximadamente ocho años. Había estado lejos de mi hogar por tanto tiempo y solo quería estar en casa en Los Ángeles. Me uní a mi amigo Louis D'Esposito, en una película que quedó estancada por razones creativas, y Lou iba a hacer otra película y me pidió que me uniera. "¿No quieres saber qué es?" me preguntó. Le dije que no me importaba. Mientras fuera rodada en Los Ángeles, yo me apuntaba. Esa película era IRON MAN.

Antes de que termináramos con IRON MAN, Kevin Feige nos ofreció a Lou y a mí unirnos a lo que se convertiría en el futuro hogar del Marvel Cinematic Universe. Kevin quería que los tres siguiéramos haciendo películas juntos en lo que tiempo después llegaría a ser Marvel Studios.

Le dije que estaba dispuesta a unirme si pudiera estar a cargo tanto de los efectos visuales como de todo el proceso de post-producción. De esa manera, el potencial conflicto entre editorial y efectos visuales tendría que desaparecer para que estas películas funcionaran de manera eficiente y contaran las mejores historias posibles. Tuvimos que unificarnos y tener una voz guiándonos y protegiendo constantemente solo lo que fuera mejor para la película, y no la agenda personal de algún individuo y así lo hicimos.

Este prólogo sirve como mi respuesta a esa invitación. Más de diez años han pasado y hemos tenido la fortuna de presentarle al mundo una colección de héroes interconectados y en constante crecimiento. La complejidad y la pura suerte de todo esto realmente no registran hasta que exploras un libro como este. Las imágenes de este diccionario visual de Marvel Studios son un recordatorio de cada una de las decisiones creativas que tuvieron que tomarse para cumplir con la fecha de lanzamiento de una película, sí, pero aún más importante es que tuvieron que tomarse conforme a lo que sería mejor para los personajes.

"¿Para quién crees que trabajas?"
Es una de las cosas que siempre digo cuando entrevisto a gente que vienen a trabajar para nosotros. Por supuesto, están nerviosos y la respuesta natural suele ser, "Eh ... ¿tú?"
No.
"Marvel Studios?"
Tampoco.
Y les digo la respuesta, en términos muy claros: "trabajas para Iron Man. Trabajas para la Capitán Marvel. Trabajas para los Guardianes. Trabajas para Black Panther. Thor. El Capitán América. El Doctor Strange. Ese es tu jefe. El jefe es la franquicia."

Después de todo, hemos visto generación tras generación de personas que se han inspirado con nuestros personajes de Marvel. Ese es el legado— y es uno que nunca se nos escapa— cuando estamos trabajando en las películas. Y creo que todo es por el espíritu humano. Eso es lo único que nos va a ayudar a prevalecer.

Todos los niños merecen verse a sí mismos en nuestras películas, independientemente de cómo se vean, sin importar de dónde vengan, sin importar el idioma que hablen, su religión, color de su piel, o cualquier otra cosa. Todos deberían tener el poder de imaginar que pueden ser un súper héroe, que pueden salvar el mundo. Esperamos poder encender ese sueño en ellos. En TODOS ellos.

De cualquier modo, tengo que irme. El 'jefe' está llamando, hasta pronto.

VICTORIA ALONSO, Vicepresidente Ejecutivo de Producción Física, Marvel Studios

CAPTAIN AMERICA

Captain America is a Super Hero, icon, wartime warrior, and leader of the Avengers. As the world's first Super-Soldier, he fights the evil Red Skull and his Hydra soldiers across the battlefields of World War II. Frozen in time for nearly 70 years, Cap emerges into the chaotic, technologically advanced world of the 21st century. Here, he finds new friends and allies in his fellow Avengers, but also new foes, and painful moral dilemmas that not even a Super-Soldier is prepared for.

"I DON'T WANT TO KILL ANYONE. I DON'T LIKE BULLIES. I DON'T CARE WHERE THEY'RE FROM."

STEVE ROGERS

STEVE ROGERS

As a small and sickly kid from Brooklyn, New York, Steve Rogers sympathizes with people who are too weak to defend themselves. After the bombing of Pearl Harbor in 1941, he is determined to enlist in the military and asks his friend Bucky Barnes to help him train in preparation for the physical exam. Steve is downhearted when Bucky is drafted, while he himself is rejected due to health problems. Rogers isn't the type of person to give up, though, even in the face of seemingly insurmountable odds. He decides to keep trying, even at the risk of being arrested for falsifying his recruitment application.

STEVE AND BUCKY

Steve Rogers and Bucky Barnes are best friends. The larger Bucky has been helping Rogers with bullies ever since they were kids. When Steve's mother died, Bucky asked Steve to come and stay with him. They are inseparable, until World War II intervenes.

Local movie theaters show propaganda films with news from the battlefront, encouraging young men to enlist, and other patriotic citizens to contribute in any way they can. Rogers has no time for those who would heckle the short war film.

At the World Exposition of Tomorrow, a dazzling showcase of futuristic technology, Rogers can't help but be drawn to the U.S. Armed Forces recruitment center. He says goodbye to Bucky and tries to enlist yet again.

Face based on Flagg's own

UNCLE SAM

The "I Want You" poster is one of 46 propaganda posters created by artist James Montgomery Flagg for the U.S. government's war effort in World War I. The iconic image is then adapted and used again for recruitment centers during World War II.

I WANT YOU FOR U.S. ARMY
NEAREST RECRUITING STATION

DESIRE TO SERVE

Steve Rogers watches all the young men around him going off to war and laying down their lives. Now his best friend is going away too. Rogers believes he has no right to do any less than them. He isn't satisfied to just stay at home and collect scrap metal for the war effort. Rogers' health problems seem insurmountable, though. He has had asthma, scarlet fever, and rheumatic fever, and suffers from sinusitis, chronic colds, high blood pressure, heart palpitations, and fatigue—and he's just too small.

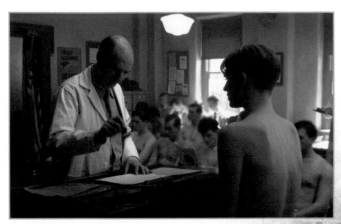

TRAINING FOR WAR

On June 14, 1943, after the intervention of scientist Dr. Abraham Erskine, Steve Rogers is finally accepted into the U.S. Army. Rogers trains in the Strategic Scientific Reserve (S.S.R.) Super-Soldier program at Camp Lehigh in New Jersey. He faces taunting and sabotage from fellow program members, while Colonel Chester Phillips, the program's military commander, is skeptical of Rogers' subpar physical abilities. Dr. Erskine insists it is his other attributes—honor, self-sacrifice, and perseverance—that make Steve the best possible candidate.

Undaunted by the terrible casualties in Europe, or the many times he is rejected, Steve Rogers tries to enlist five times in five cities; each time under a different fake residence. Yet each time, his application is stamped "4-F"—unfit.

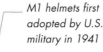

M1 helmets first adopted by U.S. military in 1941

U.S. Army wool field shirt

M1 Garand rifle is U.S. Army standard-issue

DATA FILE

> Rogers' parents both died helping others: his father while serving in World War I, and his mother after contracting tuberculosis as a nurse.

> On his enlistment forms, Rogers lists fake addresses in Connecticut, Pennsylvania, Massachusetts, New York, and New Jersey.

Dr. Erskine is scientific director of the Super-Soldier program (a.k.a. Project Rebirth). He is drawn to Rogers because of his persistence and desire to serve despite his size. Erskine has the authority to overrule the recruitment doctors, and so has Rogers accepted into the army and Project Rebirth.

TEST SUBJECT
Dr. Erskine hopes he has finally perfected the Super-Soldier Serum. If so, it will do more than make Steve Rogers stronger—it will amplify his moral character too—turning a good man like Rogers into a great one.

PROJECT REBIRTH

During World War II, the U.S. military's Strategic Scientific Reserve (S.S.R.) launches a desperate program called Project Rebirth: a plan to defeat the Nazis by creating an army of Super-Soldiers. These soldiers would possess superior physical attributes and moral character. The operation is overseen by Col. Chester Phillips, Agent Peggy Carter, and the kindly Dr. Abraham Erskine. German Dr. Erskine is the inventor of the Super-Soldier Serum and the sole guardian of its formula. He recruits Steve Rogers into the program, and Rogers undergoes Erskine's top-secret treatment, transforming him from a frail young man into the pinnacle of human physical development.

Genius inventor Howard Stark mans the controls for the Rebirth pod and monitors the Vita-Ray levels. At 70 percent, Rogers starts screaming, but bravely insists that they keep going.

"Do not touch when in use"

VITA-RAY INDICATOR

The S.S.R.'s secret Project Rebirth laboratory is located under an antiques store in Brooklyn, New York. Howard Stark's company has built all of the equipment in the lab. Observers, including Col. Phillips, Fred Clemson (secretly Heinz Kruger, an agent of the Nazi science division Hydra), and Senator Brandt, watch from a viewing booth.

DR. ERSKINE

Dr. Erskine's research into creating super-humans caught the attention of Hydra leader Johann Schmidt, and he was taken into custody. He was rescued from captivity and recruited to develop his formula for the U.S. military.

Secret formula is kept chilled

VIAL OF SUPER-SOLDIER SERUM

BECOMING A SUPER-SOLDIER

Steve Rogers lies down in the Rebirth pod and is given a shot of penicillin. Next, he receives seven simultaneous microinjections of the Super-Soldier Serum into his major muscle groups. This causes immediate cellular change (and significant discomfort). The pod is then stood vertically and closed before Rogers is saturated with Vita-Rays—a rare, exotic form of radiation—to stimulate growth. Fortunately this final step lasts only one minute, as it is extremely painful.

Arms monitor vitals and restrain Rogers

Hatch swings forward to close

Super-Soldier Serum infusers

Lead-lined hull prevents Vita-Ray leakage

Vita-Ray emitters line inside of pod

"CAPTAIN AMERICA"

Steve Rogers' transformation is nearly instantaneous and very dramatic. Before, he weighed just 95 lbs (43 kg) and was 5 ft 4 in (1.6 m) tall. When he emerges from the Rebirth pod he is 240 lbs (109 kg) and 6 ft 2 in (1.9 m) tall. He is now at peak physical performance, capable of chasing automobiles and lifting thousands of pounds. Rogers is intended to be the first of many such Super-Soldiers, but when Heinz Kruger assassinates Dr. Erskine in the lab, the formula—which exists only in Erskine's memory—is lost.

Scrawny muscles have grown massive

Even bones in hands have grown

Baggy pants have filled out

Drawings reflect Rogers' discontent

Anxious to serve, Rogers accepts Senator Brandt's proposal to send him on a War Bonds tour of the country. The "Star-Spangled Man With A Plan" is nervous on stage at first, but quickly gains confidence.

DATA FILE

> Rogers was born on July 4, 1918, and was given a patriotic upbringing.

> Captain America is a big hit with wartime kids. He features in a series of films, comic books, and collectors' cards.

> War Bonds are sold to finance the U.S. war effort with voluntary investments (rather than taxes) totaling $185 billion.

CAP SALUTES YOU!

for Buying
WAR BONDS
SEE YOUR LOCAL POST OFFICE

In Italy, Rogers has uncomfortable experiences on stage during a morale-boosting tour for frontline troops. He feels like he is just pretending to be a soldier in front of real war heroes. Rogers retreats to the solace of his art between shows.

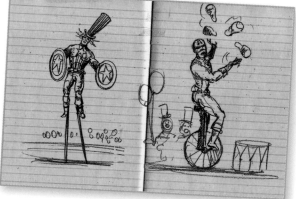

STEVE'S SKETCHBOOK

Steve Rogers is a talented amateur artist and even took art classes before volunteering for Project Rebirth. During his tour, Rogers uses art to explore his frustrations about being used as a War Bonds mascot. Originally he hoped he would be fighting on the battlefield, but in reality he is just a trained performer.

CAPTAIN AMERICA

Captain America has super-strength, speed, agility, and a strategic mind. He is a born leader with moral fortitude and the ability to bring out the best in his allies. He fights in World War II as if he is invincible, even though he isn't. Captain America is still a mortal man, but his courage and the strength of his convictions means that he doesn't fear death. He believes freedom and liberty are ideals worth dying for.

HELMET
The wings on Cap's battle helmet are a nod to his original tour costume. The form-fitting design means he can get into fistfights without it getting knocked off.

Bulletproof helmet

Carbon polymer flame-resistant jacket

Vibranium shield provided by Howard Stark

STEEL SHIELD

Cap's first shield is merely a prop from his tour costume. Its steel body makes it bulletproof, but it is not designed for battle.

Army Air Corps AN-6530 goggles

IMPROVISED GEAR
Captain America's first battle is a solo mission to rescue his captured friend, Bucky Barnes. Cap doesn't yet have a battle-ready suit, so he throws a leather jacket over his tour costume, and steals one of the tour showgirls' helmets.

FIRST SUPER-SOLDIER
Cap's first task in the war is that of a glorified mascot, touring the frontlines to boost morale. When he finally gets the chance to prove himself, he leads his team of Howling Commandos in battles against the rogue Nazi science division, Hydra. Cap is motivated by patriotism, duty, and a desire to help the oppressed. He always leads from the front, willing to sacrifice himself to save the lives of his troops. His fearlessness is infamous among Hydra soldiers, raising terror in their ranks whenever they see his red-white-and-blue shield.

Unpainted vibranium

CAP'S SHIELD
The inventor Howard Stark makes several shield prototypes for Cap to try. Some include electroshock relays and other built-in gadgetry, but Cap is drawn to a simple round shield composed of multiple layers of rare vibranium metal. It doesn't just deflect projectiles—it is also resistant to extreme heat.

Hydra soldiers carry supercharged energy weapons and oversized flamethrowers. Cap's shield is essential protection against these weapons.

Custom-fitted blue-dyed U.S. paratrooper pants

Paratrooper jump boots

Cap successfully rescues Bucky (and 162 other prisoners) from a Hydra weapons facility. As they escape the burning factory, Cap and Bucky run into the fleeing Hydra leader, Johann Schmidt, a.k.a. Red Skull. The enemies' first encounter is a forerunner of future bitter clashes.

Ridged for extra grip when throwing shield

Ammo pouch

UTILITY BELT

Holds a Colt M1911A1 handgun

HOLSTER

COMBAT GLOVES

CAP'S EQUIPMENT

Captain America's equipment is custom tailored for him at Howard Stark's S.S.R. lab in London. Most of it is standard WWII-era gear with size adjustments for Steve Rogers' large frame and bolstered for increased durability. Some of the gadgets in his belt are cutting-edge tech, like location transponders that allow Cap to call for extraction, mini-bombs, and exploding bullets.

Rear flamethrower

Tripwire/tow cable launcher

Slot for Cap's shield

Missile launcher

Holster for rifle or shotgun

Reinforced footrest

CUSTOM MOTORCYCLE

Captain America drives a 1942 Harley-Davidson WLA "Liberator" with customizations made by Howard Stark. It is designed for battling Hydra vehicles while driving, and includes a handy self-destruct feature.

Cap and the Howling Commandos have remarkable success as they turn each enemy base into rubble. Cap becomes a national symbol, inspiring other U.S. soldiers and their families back home.

In his final wartime mission, Cap seizes control of a Hydra bomber bound for America with weapons of mass destruction aboard. He bravely chooses to crash the plane into the Arctic ice rather than risk civilian lives by flying over land. Cap and the plane lie untouched in the ice for almost 70 years.

BUCKY BARNES

Sergeant James Buchanan "Bucky" Barnes is a childhood friend of Steve Rogers. He is charming, patriotic, and fiercely loyal to those he considers friends. Drafted into the army after the attack on Pearl Harbor, he trains at Camp McCoy, Wisconsin, and in 1943 heads to Europe to join the fight against the Nazis. Shortly afterward, his unit is attacked at Azzano, Italy, and he is taken prisoner by the rogue Nazi research division, Hydra. Bucky and the other prisoners are rescued by Captain America, and he joins Cap's new commando unit, taking part in attacks on Hydra facilities across Europe. On a mission in 1945, he is knocked from a Hydra train and listed as killed in action—but in reality, his fate is much worse.

Well-tended hair, even in battle

Wool naval peacoat for cool weather

Leather holster for .45 pistol

Colt M1911A1 sidearm

STEVE'S BEST FRIEND

Bucky Barnes was born on March 10, 1917, making him just over a year older than his best friend, Steve Rogers. Bucky provided emotional support to young Steve when his mother died from tuberculosis, and physical support when Steve was picked on. Later, Bucky, himself a three-time YMCA welterweight champion, trained Steve in preparation for his first application to the army. Steve was devastated when Bucky was drafted and he thought he couldn't follow, and mourned Bucky when he believed he had died during their final mission together.

Bucky's easy-going personality and sense of humor make him popular with women. He wears his Class A dress uniform on his last night before going off to war, hoping to impress his date.

Before Bucky's 107th Infantry Division ships out to England the following day, he and Steve visit the 1943 World Exposition of Tomorrow in New York City, with their dates, Connie and Bonnie. Steve leaves them to try to enlist once more, and will not see Bucky again until they meet in Austria.

Steve Rogers, now the Super-Soldier known as Captain America, rescues Bucky and other Allied prisoners from a Hydra weapons factory located between Klagenfurt and Kitzbühel in the Austrian Alps. During this incarceration, Bucky is experimented on by Hydra scientist Dr. Zola, which has unknown effects on Bucky's body.

Baggy U.S. paratrooper pants

Leather U.S. paratrooper jump boots with M1938 dismounted leggings

BUCKY'S THOMPSON
SUBMACHINE GUN

Recoil
compensator

Rear sight

Butt stock

Fore grip

Bullet magazine
contains 30 rounds

Safety catch

Carrying strap

HOWLING COMMANDO

After rescuing Bucky and returning with the POWs to Colonel Chester Phillip's base in Italy, Steve Rogers forms a new unit to take on Hydra, known as the Howling Commandos. Bucky is surprised by the transformation that Steve has undergone, but isn't swayed by Captain America's newfound fame. He joins the "Howlers" because he remembers "that little guy from Brooklyn who was too dumb to run away from a fight." Barnes would be the only member of the unit presumed to have died in battle.

While in captivity and during the subsequent rescue, Bucky and Cap both get a look at maps showing Hydra's base locations. Bucky is tactically proficient and helps Cap plan their operations against Hydra. Such strategy meetings later appear in U.S. war propaganda films back home.

Bucky and the Howling Commandos monitor Hydra communications in preparation for a mission to capture Dr. Zola. Ironically, given Rogers' new abilities, Bucky is more at ease before battle than Captain America. This mission is the last time the friends see each other for almost 70 years.

CRACK SHOT

Bucky is an excellent marksman and often serves as a sniper for the Howling Commandos. While Cap takes on Hydra soldiers up close, Bucky crouches from afar with a customized semi-automatic M1941 Johnson rifle and sniper scope. His skills inspire a rumor among Hydra infantry that soldiers drop dead as Captain America approaches them.

Coating reduces
reflections

PEGGY CARTER

Perceptive, principled, and steadfast in the face of adversity, Peggy Carter is an agent in the Strategic Scientific Reserve (S.S.R.), and a loyal wartime colleague of Steve Rogers. Carter was born in London, England, and served in the Royal Air Force and Special Air Service before joining the S.S.R. in 1940. A highly valued agent, Carter is known for her astute leadership, tactical skills, and resourceful attitude. Peggy is a key player in the Allies' intelligence network, and also an early champion of Rogers' ability to bear the Captain America mantle.

Carter befriends Steve Rogers, viewing him to be the best candidate for Project Rebirth, despite his physical limitations. His compassion for others and selflessness are key attributes for the role.

SECRET AGENT

Working for British Secret Intelligence as "Agent 13," Carter infiltrates Hydra's Castle Kaufmann base and obtains footage of its secret weapons shipments. This is shared with American Intelligence, and the U.S. government's S.S.R. then assists Carter in rescuing the renowned German scientist Dr. Erskine, who is being held captive by Hydra. Both Carter and Erskine subsequently join the S.S.R. and Project Rebirth. Alongside Colonel Phillips, Carter oversees the S.S.R.'s Super-Soldier training program and subsequent commando offensive against Hydra.

Newspaper clipping of Peggy's photograph

STEVE ROGERS' COMPASS

S.S.R. pin

Proudly worn uniform of smartly tailored skirt suit

Golden buttons always polished

Agent Carter oversees the training of Project Rebirth candidates at Camp Lehigh. Throughout her early career she is the recipient of sexist treatment from both subordinates and superiors, as well as snide comments about her British origin.

DATA FILE

> Agent Carter carries a Walther PPK pistol, which she uses to stop the getaway driver of Hydra assassin Heinz Kruger. The pistol is her signature firearm, even during her time at S.H.I.E.L.D.

> Peggy is a skilled hand-to-hand combatant, having learned a range of different fighting techniques over the years.

> Carter's husband was one of the thousands saved by Steve Rogers during World War II.

Hair styled
in pin curls

Agent Carter is an accomplished markswoman, and she doesn't take a back seat on missions. Armed with her Thompson submachine gun, she leads the Howling Commandos into Hydra's headquarters in the Alps. She continues to lead such dangerous missions throughout her S.H.I.E.L.D. career.

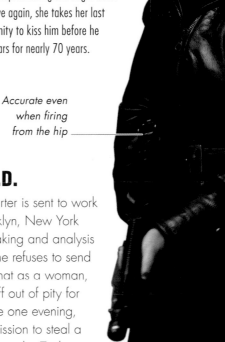

Peggy has strong feelings for Steve Rogers, but their duties are an obstacle to a romantic relationship. Knowing she might never see Steve again, she takes her last opportunity to kiss him before he disappears for nearly 70 years.

Accurate even
when firing
from the hip

FOUNDING S.H.I.E.L.D.

After World War II, Agent Carter is sent to work at S.S.R. headquarters in Brooklyn, New York City. She is assigned code-breaking and analysis duties by Agent John Flynn, but he refuses to send her on field missions, believing that as a woman, she has only been kept on staff out of pity for her loss of Steve Rogers. Late one evening, however, she takes on a mission to steal a chemical weapon known as the Zodiac. After she succeeds, Flynn receives a call from Howard Stark, notifying him that Carter will help run the new intelligence agency, S.H.I.E.L.D.

Simple, but stylish,
professional attire

Peggy Carter remains at S.H.I.E.L.D., and conducts herself honorably even while it is gradually corrupted from within by Hydra. She oversees Hank Pym's field missions as Ant-Man, and is unhappy when she discovers that her colleagues Howard Stark and Mitchell Carson are conspiring against Pym.

Carter struggles with Alzheimer's in her later years and she passes away aged 98. Her funeral is held at her favorite London cathedral. Attendees include former S.H.I.E.L.D. agents, various dignitaries, her great-niece Sharon Carter, and Steve Rogers.

RED SKULL

Johann Schmidt is an ambitious German scientist and Nazi officer preoccupied with Norse mythology and unearthly powers. As a promising youth, the Nazis spot his potential and the leader of their security force, the Schutzstaffel (S.S.), takes Schmidt on as a protégé. Schmidt climbs up the Nazi ranks, killing Ernst Kaufmann, head of the regime's special weapons division, and taking Kaufmann's resources for his own budding science division, Hydra. Learning of Dr. Erskine's research into creating Super-Soldiers, Schmidt kidnaps him and takes the formula for himself. It bestows physical resilience and mental acuity upon Schmidt, but leaves him monstrously scarred.

Discoloration around eyes hints at red visage beneath

Nazi S.S. science officer uniform

Red piping emphasizes smart cut of jacket

Gleaming leather boots

In March 1942, Schmidt loots an old church building in Tønsberg, Norway, searching for the Tesseract—a powerful Asgardian artifact. He throws a decoy aside before uncovering the real one. The Nazis are obsessed with mystical artifacts of power, but Schmidt dismisses Hitler's searches as hunts for mere "trinkets," compared to this.

Visual representation of the powers of the Tesseract

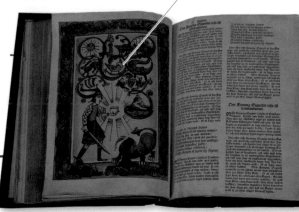

ANCIENT BOOK
An earthly version of the *Book of Yggdrasil* (minus the magical qualities) tells the story of the Nine Realms of Asgard and the history of Odin's family. Viewed as mythology by its former guardians, Schmidt uses the illuminated text to learn about the Tesseract.

Bullet magazine fits inside grip frame

SCHMIDT'S PISTOL
Schmidt carries a German Luger P08 semi-automatic pistol, popular with Nazi officers. Later, chief Hydra scientist Dr. Arnim Zola creates a new Luger-inspired weapon powered by Tesseract energy to replace it.

HYDRA LEADER
After the incident with the Super-Soldier Serum, Schmidt wears a mask to hide his scarred face. He resents Hitler and the Nazis for marginalizing him, seeing them as small-minded and primitive. Where they see magic, he sees science, and with it the power to conquer and reshape the world. He inspires his men with quantifiable results, whereas Hitler can't even keep his army fed. Schmidt rapidly raises Hydra from a small research department to a military organization rivaling the Nazi Party.

Head disfigured by unproven Super-Soldier Serum

TESSERACT WEAPONS

Once he acquires the Tesseract, Schmidt sets Dr. Arnim Zola to work using its energy to power his inventions. Some are modifications to existing weapons, others are new designs. When Nazi officials demand a demonstration, Schmidt delights in vaporizing them with his new cannon.

Cold-energy cannon

Barrel fires blue Tesseract energy

RED SKULL REVEALED

In 1943, while inspecting one of his weapons factories, Johann Schmidt encounters Captain America and Bucky Barnes. Hoping to terrify them, he takes the opportunity to reveal his shocking true face as Red Skull. Now unmasked, Red Skull boldly leads Hydra with renewed vigor. However, as Captain America and the Howling Commandos continue to gain ground in the war, Red Skull's focus shifts from Europe to a potentially catastrophic attack on America.

DATA FILE

> Red Skull strikes terror not only in the Allied forces, but in his own men—he is known to shoot officers on the spot who don't achieve his goals.

> Red Skull vanishes after grabbing the Tesseract with his bare hand. He is banished to Vormir, where he is condemned to become the guardian of the Soul Stone for decades.

Valuable silver belt buckle with Hydra emblem

Open top allows greater situational awareness

SCHMIDT'S COUPE

Schmidt's custom car makes a statement. The design looks great in parades, impresses factory management when he arrives, and elicits jealousy in his colleagues. The powerful engine and armored body also let him drive through battle zones.

FRONT VIEW

Extra gauges for Tesseract-powered engine

Leather trench coat, part of Hydra uniform

HYDRA

Hydra begins as the deep-science division of the Nazi Schutzstaffel (S.S.), which itself is the most powerful organization in Nazi Germany, infamous for its surveillance, security apparatus, and implementation of terror. Hydra is founded by Johann Schmidt (later known as Red Skull) with the backing of the S.S. leadership. Under Schmidt's command, Hydra builds an army to rival Hitler's and breaks away from the regime with its own rival plan for world domination. Schmidt's ambition frightens even the Nazis. As Nazi Germany wanes, Hydra appears to be on the verge of replacing it.

Dr. Zola works tirelessly in his lab, putting the Tesseract's limitless energy to use in his futuristic inventions. He relishes the chance to create new technology, and doesn't care about the horrific uses his creations are put to.

ZOLANATOR 2000X ASSAULT RIFLE

Ammunition magazine

Forward pistol grip

Tentacles represent Hydra's invasive reach

Wide-brimmed fedora

HYDRA SYMBOL

HYDRA TROOPS
The soldiers of Hydra are fanatical. They worship Red Skull like a cult leader, swearing complete loyalty to him and the organization. Most are former Nazi soldiers who relish Red Skull's vision of world order through glorious technological might.

Goggles reduce glare from energy weapons

DR. ARNIM ZOLA
Dr. Arnim Zola is a brilliant Hydra scientist and second-in-command to Johann Schmidt. Thanks to Zola's innovations with an otherworldly artifact named the Tesseract, Hydra's technology is decades ahead of the Allies. Following the destruction of Hydra's weapons factories by Cap and his Howling Commandos, Zola eventually sells Schmidt out to the Allies to save himself, and then rebuilds Hydra to his own design.

Hydra pin

Pouches for power cell ammunition

Arnimhilation 99L assault weapon

FIESER DORSCH MINI SUBMARINE

Hook for crane lift

Cockpit with reinforced glass

Vertical stabilizer

Bow hydroplane

Hydropulse engine pod

Propeller removed for maintenance

HYDRA VEHICLES

Hydra's vehicles are all man-made technology with arcane influences: Common machines that have been upgraded using energy and materials derived from the Tesseract. These upgrades include advanced propulsion systems, miniaturized power sources, and devastating energy weapons.

Intended target is painted on craft's front

HYDRA PARASIT

Johann Schmidt's Parasits are essentially flying bombs with more destructive power than a nuclear weapon. They each require one suicide bomber pilot to operate. The craft are carried in groups of eight aboard the super-bomber *Valkyrie*, with the intention of launching them over America.

Deep treads for rough forest tracks

Driver's seat (no passengers)

Aerial for communications

Grendel 900 heavy cannon

LINDWORM-5 MOTORCYCLE

Hydra's combat motorcycles are covered in reinforced armor and equipped with a pair of energy cannons. They are used to patrol roads leading to Hydra's bases, making them hazardous for Allied forces. Their "Lindworm" name is inspired by the Germanic dragon, due to their occasional habit of spontaneously bursting into flames.

DATA FILE

> The Hydra salute involves raising both arms and shouting "Hail Hydra!"

> Before the end of the war, Hydra cells infiltrate the Soviet Union.

HYDRA TANK

Based on the German army's Leichter Panzerspähwagen series of armored cars, the Hydra tank has the addition of a powerful energy weapon that can melt through the thickest armor of Allied vehicles. However, its many blind spots make it vulnerable to infantry.

HOWLING COMMANDOS

Captain America's personal unit during World War II is known as the Howling Commandos. Aside from his old friend Bucky Barnes, Cap first meets the brave men who will join his team when he rescues them from a prison inside a Hydra weapons facility. He forms the unit shortly afterward, and leads them in covert attacks on Hydra throughout occupied Europe. Despite Hydra's superior technology, the team wages a successful campaign. Their ultimate victory is bittersweet, however, with the loss of both Bucky and Cap.

The Howling Commandos' operations are coordinated from the European headquarters of the Strategic Scientific Reserve (S.S.R.), a bunker on King Charles Street in London. Colonel Phillips and Agent Carter both have offices here, and Howard Stark has an adjoining laboratory.

Trademark Dum Dum mustache

Innovative "bullpup" rifle design (magazine is placed behind trigger)

U.S. Army knitted wool jeep cap

Good trigger discipline

After their rescue, the future Howlers head to London to recover. At the *Whip & Fiddle* pub, Captain America asks them to join his team. Falsworth is the first to join, because it sounds "fun." Dum Dum is the last to agree, insisting on unlimited drinks first.

Wool army pants

DUM DUM'S BOWLER HAT

Brim has seen better days

Hydra Zolanator 2000X assault rifle

HYDRA'S NIGHTMARE

After infiltrating a Hydra base, Cap discovers map locations for all of Hydra's facilities. He puts the Howling Commandos together to systematically attack every Hydra stronghold in Europe. One by one they destroy each base, even capturing Arnim Zola, right-hand man of Hydra leader Johann Schmidt, though they lose Bucky in the process. Zola gives them the location of Schmidt's secret headquarters, leading to a final assault. Schmidt flees with Cap in pursuit, but both men then vanish, leaving the Howlers to mourn their fallen leader.

JIM MORITA

Japanese-American Jim Morita is from Fresno, California. As the team's radio operator and tech expert, he studies Hydra equipment and intercepts their communications.

JACQUES DERNIER

Former French Resistance fighter Jacques Dernier was captured in Marseilles before meeting the other Howling Commandos. He is the team's explosives expert.

DUM DUM DUGAN

Tough New Yorker Timothy "Dum Dum" Dugan is a close friend of Bucky Barnes. He takes on a leadership role after Bucky and Captain America disappear in 1945.

EQUIPPING THE COMMANDOS

Howard Stark develops equipment for the Howling Commandos at his S.S.R. laboratory. There he designs prototype shields for Captain America, as well as special armaments for their missions. Stark studies the Hydra technology the commandos seize; when its unearthly Tesseract energy proves too volatile to use, retrieving the Tesseract itself becomes Howard's obsession.

Magnetic plate

Explosive canister

TRACK BOMB

Howard Stark creates this stable portable magnetic bomb for the commandos to attach to Hydra vehicles. Jacques Dernier is most comfortable with explosives, so he usually volunteers for the job.

Maroon British paratrooper beret

U.S. Infantry garrison cap

Captain America allows himself to be captured, and the Howling Commandos follow him into Hydra's Alpine headquarters. They face off against Hydra's elite soldiers in the technologically advanced facility, hoping to capture Schmidt and bring an end to Hydra.

Hydra Arnimhilation 99L assault weapon

Leather paratrooper boots

DATA FILE

> Dum Dum continues to serve his country after the war, first via the S.S.R. and then as part of counter-terrorism agency S.H.I.E.L.D.

> Falsworth is one of the most decorated Howlers, receiving the African Star, Order of Burma, Defense Medal, and War Medal.

> Bucky is the only member of the unit who is listed as killed in action.

JAMES MONTGOMERY FALSWORTH

James Montgomery Falsworth is an expert strategist. He served in His Majesty's 3rd Independent Parachute Regiment before he was captured by Hydra.

BUCKY BARNES

James Buchanan Barnes is the Howling Commandos' sniper. He and Steve Rogers have been inseparable friends since 1930.

GABE JONES

Howard University student Gabe Jones is from Macon, Georgia. He speaks German and French, and is the Howlers' heavy weapons specialist.

CAP'S UNIFORMS

Nearly 70 years after Captain America is lost in the Arctic, his plane is discovered and his body is brought to S.H.I.E.L.D. headquarters. After he is thawed out, Rogers has a tumultuous adjustment to present-day life. He is quickly thrown back into battle in New York, now as leader of the Avengers. Once the dust settles he is left feeling lonely and isolated—everyone from his past is now in a nursing home or deceased. Hydra then re-emerges to torment him, and finally the Avengers collapse into civil war. Through it all, the only things Cap can rely on are his patriotic uniforms and shield.

The Super-Soldier Serum in Rogers' body allows him to survive decades in frozen hibernation. He wakes up in an unfamiliar century, in a country that has experienced huge cultural shifts since his time. For Cap, the shock of such change is profound.

Avengers transceiver embedded in cowl

Red-and-white motif continues on arms

Shield attaches magnetically to forearm

AVENGERS UNIFORM

Stars and stripes design

Cap's first modern uniform is created by S.H.I.E.L.D., with design tweaks suggested by Agent Phil Coulson. It is based on his 1940s outfit, with new stretch fabric that is even stronger than the old material. His vibranium shield is the same one given to him by Howard Stark during World War II.

Not only is Cap dealing with an unfamiliar future—he must cope with hostile aliens, too. Fortunately his high-tech blast-resistant vest can absorb hits from Chitauri weapons.

Pouches hold medical kit for wounded civilians

New form-fitting armored cowl

Strap for shield rig on back

SOKOVIA UNIFORM

After the fall of S.H.I.E.L.D., inventor Tony Stark takes over designing Captain America's outfits. Cap now fully embraces his role as Avengers leader, so the red-white-and-blue colors return. Some stealthy features from his previous uniform are retained though, giving him an edge in field missions.

Heavy boots suited to rubble of urban war zone

As part of S.H.I.E.L.D.'s STRIKE team, Cap fights the French-Algerian mercenary Georges Batroc (nicknamed "Batroc the Leaper") in hand-to-hand combat aboard the hijacked ship *Lemurian Star*.

STEALTH UNIFORM

Cap has another new uniform created when he joins S.H.I.E.L.D.'s special forces STRIKE team. The colors are more subdued for stealthy nighttime missions. Sometimes his shield is also painted a monochromatic blue to draw less attention. This suit identifies Cap more as a member of S.H.I.E.L.D. than an Avenger.

Loose pants with reinforced kneepads

In Sokovia, Steve Rogers finds himself back where his journey as Captain America started, on a motorcycle in Europe, being fired at by Hydra soldiers with energy weapons. He wears his shield on his back for protection at the cost of leaving his front exposed.

NEW AVENGERS UNIFORM

Captain America's latest uniform is more lightweight, but actually has more substantial armor built into the clothing than his previous suit. This comes in handy for missions against heavily armed terrorists. Though his suit is durable, maneuverability means a balance must be struck; Cap's uniform isn't bombproof! Fellow Avenger Scarlet Witch is aware of this, so she rushes to save him when the terrorist known as Crossbones sets off a suicide bomb.

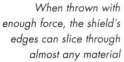

When thrown with enough force, the shield's edges can slice through almost any material

Cap's main vulnerability is his legs. They are not well protected and Cap is top-heavy, so if an opponent is skillful (and lucky) Cap can be knocked over.

Red details on chest and white arm stripes are now blue

Woloski 200 satellite communicator in pouch

Shock absorption kneepad

In Lagos, Nigeria, Captain America confronts his old S.H.I.E.L.D. colleague, Brock Rumlow, now the terrorist Crossbones. Rumlow blames Cap for his scarred face and lasting injuries received during the collapse of S.H.I.E.L.D.'s headquarters. Obsessed with revenge, Rumlow plans to kill Cap and himself.

Wide pockets carry field gear

Armored gaiters protect lower legs

DATA FILE

> Cap's shield is even able to resist a blow from Thor's hammer, Mjolnir. However, such an impact creates a devastating sonic shockwave.

> Cap and Thor sometimes take advantage of the shield/Mjolnir shockwave effect to stun nearby enemies and throw them off balance.

FALCON

|||||||||||||||||||||||||||||||||||||||||||||||||||||||||||||||||||

Sam Wilson is both the high-flying master of the skies known as Falcon, and a stalwart friend of Steve Rogers. A former U.S. Air Force pararescue officer who retired from active duty to work at Veterans Affairs (V.A.), Wilson helps fellow veterans suffering from Post-Traumatic Stress Disorder. Sam's aerial acrobatics come courtesy of a powerful jetpack that allows him to swoop into action at eye-watering speeds. A wise-cracking but focused soldier, he follows Cap through thick and thin, aiding in struggles with Hydra and the corrupted S.H.I.E.L.D., before officially joining the Avengers' roster—and later leaving it as a fugitive in solidarity with Cap.

Sam Wilson first meets Steve Rogers when both are jogging around the National Mall in Washington D.C. Wilson laments that Rogers literally runs circles around him. While they talk, Wilson recommends post-World War II music to Rogers. They quickly become friends and Rogers accepts his invitation to visit him at the V.A.

Wings extend outward, unfolding like a hand fan

EXO-7 MARK I

THE EXO-7

Wilson's experimental winged jetpack—the EXO-7 Falcon—is developed by the U.S. Air National Guard. Wilson and his wingman Riley are the original test pilots. Sam retires from the program after Riley is killed in action in Afghanistan, but retrieves his EXO-7 from storage when Cap and Black Widow ask for help. The EXO-7 backpack boasts three miniature jet engines, composite wings that collapse and compress inside the pack for storage, and an emergency parachute.

Holster for a Steyr SPP firearm

Handlebars for steering in flight

Magnified image of Ant-Man

Real-time map of Avengers compound

Reinforced kneepads for tough landings

After Hydra re-emerges from within S.H.I.E.L.D., Falcon uses his EXO-7 to board Hydra's new Helicarriers to try and disable them. Falcon's pack is fast enough to evade a pursuing Quinjet, but the Hydra operative known as the Winter Soldier de-wings him, forcing Falcon to parachute to safety.

Lenses have built-in augmented reality display

COMBAT GOGGLES

Falcon flies at very high speeds, so eye protection is vital. His original goggles have a basic zoom function, but he later receives upgraded examples from Tony Stark. These include a visual interface that links to Redwing, allowing him to see through the drone's eyes in a variety of spectra, detect heat signatures, and search using pattern recognition algorithms.

Falcon's ultra-flexible wings are bulletproof, and can wrap around him to form a near-full body shield against bullets, shrapnel, minor explosions, and flames. These features allow him to drop into the middle of intense combat without needing to seek cover.

Jointed mechanical arm brace

DATA FILE

> Wilson is the first Avenger to meet Scott Lang (Ant-Man) when Scott infiltrates the Avengers facility. Sam later nicknames him "Tic Tac."

> Officially, Redwing is the "Stark Drone MK82 922 V 80Z V2 Prototype Unit V6."

> Redwing is equipped with a video camera, twin guns, a retractable tow cable, and stun missile.

Smart goggles linked to Redwing

Nylon reinforced Mylar vanes

Gauntlet with Redwing touch-pad controls

WINGED WARRIOR

Wilson's equipment is upgraded when he joins the Avengers. His left gauntlet bears a double-barreled wrist-mounted machine gun, while the right has a miniature rocket launcher. Sam can fire both by clenching his fists. The Redwing drone can be launched as a projectile, too. Wilson's EXO-7 Mark II backpack includes miniature guided missiles, with targeting controlled via Redwing. The reinforced wings can also be used as melee weapons.

Falcon aids the Winter Soldier and Captain America in the Avengers' internal conflict over the Sokovia Accords. He uses his Redwing drone to search for a S.H.I.E.L.D. Quinjet at Leipzig-Halle Airport, hoping to board it and escape.

EXO-7 MARK II

Redwing activates by voice command, "Redwing launch"

REDWING

Redwing is the latest addition to Falcon's gear. The advanced drone was developed by Stark Industries and allows Wilson to survey the ground less conspicuously, since his own EXO-7 throws a much larger shadow. The drone is carried on Wilson's back for field deployment.

Retractable wing

One of two gun hatches

HYDRA UPRISING

Captain America's old nemesis Hydra rears its head again when it emerges like a parasite from the heart of S.H.I.E.L.D. Dr. Arnim Zola has been secretly rebuilding Hydra for 70 years, slowly poisoning S.H.I.E.L.D. from the inside. Infiltrating every level of the organization—from field agents to Alexander Pierce, Secretary of the World Security Council—Hydra's followers work toward a secret project for the ultimate elimination of all opposition to its global conquest.

Bulletproof vest

Green-and-yellow STRIKE emblem

BROCK RUMLOW

Brock Rumlow is leader of STRIKE, S.H.I.E.L.D.'s elite counterterrorism unit, and has worked alongside Cap on several missions. However, the traitorous Rumlow and his team are Hydra double agents, and do not hesitate to act when tasked by Pierce with eliminating Cap.

Special operations M4A1 carbine

Zola's dedication to furthering Hydra's supremacy has not even been halted by his own mortality. Despite the death of his body in 1972, Zola uploaded his brain into a nest of data banks, as a horrified Captain America discovers.

Dual holsters

On Tony Stark's suggestion, the old turbine technology used in S.H.I.E.L.D.'s Helicarriers has now been upgraded in favor of repulsor engines. This will keep them in perpetual suborbital flight, never needing to land.

Rumlow excels in hand-to-hand combat. Using electrified rods, he lands several painful shocks on Captain America.

PROJECT INSIGHT

Deep underneath S.H.I.E.L.D.'s headquarters, three enormous next-generation Helicarriers are being built in a secret construction site. Once launched, the ships will be synched to a network of targeting satellites, ostensibly as part of a global security system to protect Earth from terrorists. However, Pierce plans to use data from Zola to identify and predict Hydra's future enemies long before they act, and pre-emptively assassinate them with the ships' weapons. This brutal extermination will amount to twenty million people.

Heavy combat boots

Long-range precision guns can wipe out 1,000 hostiles per minute

Repulsor engine

> Sharon Carter is the great-niece of S.H.I.E.L.D. founder Agent Peggy Carter. She does not tell her colleagues this, preferring to succeed on her own merit.

> After World War II, S.H.I.E.L.D. recruited enemy scientists including Zola for their strategic value, as part of Operation Paperclip.

> Zola's brain is uploaded onto 200,000 feet of data banks, in a secret bunker under Cap's old training barracks, Camp Lehigh.

SHARON CARTER

Agent 13, a.k.a. S.H.I.E.L.D. Secret Service operative Sharon Carter, is tasked by Nicholas Fury with Cap's protection. An expert spy and quick-thinking strategist, Carter lives next door to Rogers, posing undercover as a nurse. She is thus in prime position to respond at a moment's notice to threats, such as the Winter Soldier's sniper attack on Fury. Carter's bravery and her strong belief in Rogers' good character fuels her support in his fight to destroy the Helicarriers and foil Hydra.

Purposeful
stance

S.H.I.E.L.D.
pin worn in
ironic show
of loyalty

JASPER SITWELL

Senior S.H.I.E.L.D. officer and Hydra double agent Jasper Sitwell proves his efficiency by coordinating a ruthless manhunt for Captain America. However, Sitwell's naivety and arrogance in believing he can predict the behavior of both his foes and his Hydra allies are key factors in his eventual downfall.

Jeans
suit smart
casual look

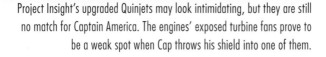

Project Insight's upgraded Quinjets may look intimidating, but they are still no match for Captain America. The engines' exposed turbine fans prove to be a weak spot when Cap throws his shield into one of them.

WINTER SOLDIER

In 1945, Howling Commando Bucky Barnes is captured by Hydra and brainwashed into becoming its secret weapon: the Winter Soldier. Now a ruthless killer who feels neither pity or fear, when he encounters Captain America almost 70 years later, the Winter Soldier sees only an enemy. Rogers desperately attempts to unlock his friend's mind and eventually breaks through. Bucky begins to re-emerge, but confusion and fragmented memories cloud his thoughts, along with the constant threat of being reawakened as Hydra's master assassin.

When scores of Hydra soldiers are unable to assassinate Nick Fury in downtown Washington D.C., the Winter Soldier steps in. He launches a disc grenade under the S.H.I.E.L.D. director's car, causing a huge explosion that flips the vehicle over.

CODEBOOK

The Winter Soldier codebook contains information vital to the program and the code phrase (spoken in Russian) to activate the Winter Soldier: "Longing, rusted, seventeen, daybreak, furnace, nine, benign, homecoming, one, freight car."

FIST OF HYDRA

Bucky falls from a train during a wartime mission to capture Hydra scientist Dr. Zola, but miraculously he survives. When he is found he is handed over to Hydra's Soviet wing, where Zola oversees Bucky's transformation into a super-assassin. He is trained to be proficient with all modern weapons, and becomes a lethal martial artist—so lethal that he is branded the "Fist of Hydra," the greatest assassin in the program. Hydra preserves its prized asset by putting him into cryogenic hibernation between missions, ironically mirroring Steve Rogers' fate.

Custom-fitted cybernetic prosthetic arm

Leather ammo pouches carry untraceable Soviet ammunition

Magnetic plate

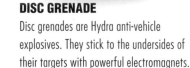

DISC GRENADE

Disc grenades are Hydra anti-vehicle explosives. They stick to the undersides of their targets with powerful electromagnets.

At first, the Winter Soldier has no recollection of Steve Rogers, nor even his own identity. He fights Rogers relentlessly with the intent to kill him. The Winter Soldier's powerful cybernetic arm is a formidable match for Cap's strength.

Bucky's left arm is torn off during his fall, but Hydra replaces it with an experimental cybernetic one. Most importantly, his mind is wiped and reprogrammed. Whenever he starts to remember fragments of his past, his mind is simply wiped again.

Grenade bursts open along seams

BALL GRENADE

Another Hydra explosive device, this ball grenade is easily rolled on smoother surfaces and has a delayed-action detonator.

Soviet 1975
pilot glove

Barnes travels to Romania to find clues about his past as a member of the Howling Commandos. While in Bucharest, Bucky learns of a bombing in Vienna— and that he is being blamed for the attack.

Electric charge in seat immobilizes Bucky's arm

Red Soviet
Communist Star

Leg shackles

CONTAINMENT CELL

After his capture in Bucharest, the Winter Soldier is placed in a special containment cell. Bucky is one of the most dangerous men alive, so the CIA will not take any chances.

Black Panther wants to kill the Winter Soldier to avenge the death of his father, King T'Chaka, in the Vienna bombing. He believes Bucky set the bomb that killed him. Fortunately, Scarlet Witch uses her powers to stop Black Panther.

Military N20
field jacket liner
with torn sleeve

Flexible material
allows for high
kicks and sprinting

Old Russian
army boots

Tony Stark is incensed when he learns that the Winter Soldier murdered his parents, Howard and Maria Stark, on Long Island in 1991. Although Bucky has no control over his actions as the Winter Soldier, he remembers every target he has ever killed, and is plagued by guilt. This is especially true regarding Howard Stark, who was Bucky's wartime friend and ally.

ON THE RUN

After S.H.I.E.L.D. falls, the Winter Soldier remembers flashes of his past and tries to piece together his old identity. He visits the Smithsonian museum's Captain America exhibit, which triggers more memories, but is forced to remain in hiding, aware that both the government and Hydra are hunting him. When a bitter Sokovian colonel named Zemo reactivates Bucky's assassin programming, however, it calls into question whether Bucky can ever truly be reformed, and forces him to flee again.

DATA FILE

> The Winter Soldier first encountered Black Widow in Iran. He shot and wounded her, and killed the scientist she was escorting.

> The Winter Soldier's high-powered firearms include a Colt M4A1 carbine assault rifle, and a selection of deadly grenade launchers.

SOKOVIA AFTERMATH

The world is tense after events in Sokovia, where an entire city is destroyed in the fight between the Avengers and the android Ultron. Public sentiment is politicized and the Avengers are scrutinized by world leaders. The heroes' missteps have resulted in dangerous weapons falling into the hands of criminals, and vengeful new nemeses arising from the collateral damage. Tony Stark's guilt over lost civilian lives weighs on him. Yet in contrast, Steve Rogers feels the Avengers have done all they can. Another horrific incident in Lagos, Nigeria, sets in motion a series of events that result in a devastating fracture in the team.

In a battle against Crossbones in Lagos, Scarlet Witch accidentally kills a group of Wakandan aid workers. For much of the world, this tragedy is the final straw.

CROSSBONES

Brock Rumlow is a former Hydra agent, once embedded within S.H.I.E.L.D. as a black-ops unit commander. He was nearly killed during the destruction of S.H.I.E.L.D.'s headquarters. His injuries left him scarred over his entire body and resulted in severe nerve damage that prevents him from feeling any pain. Rumlow, going by the moniker Crossbones, is now a notorious mercenary and arms dealer.

Nearly indestructible mask

Surplus ammunition and gauntlet attachments

Gauntlets jut out for added momentum and contain retractable blades

Mechanical force-multiplier gauntlets

Fireproof biohazard boots

THE SOKOVIA ACCORDS

After the destruction of Sokovia, and the terrible events in Lagos, the international community demands accountability—and a registration of the Avengers and other super-powered individuals. A total of 117 countries approve the U.N.-backed Sokovia Accords. U.S. Secretary of State Thaddeus Ross presents them to the Avengers.

DATA FILE

> Crossbones fires a vehicle-mounted, modified Mk 19 grenade launcher after exiting the Center for Disease Control and Prevention facility in Lagos.

> Crossbones intends to sell a biological weapon he acquires in Lagos to either The Ten Rings or Hydra—whoever pays more.

The presentation of the Sokovia Accords to the Avengers team leads to tense discussions among its members. Stark, Cap, and Vision seem to choose sides early on, while Wanda and Natasha remain more open-minded.

Clasped hands show shared affection

DEATH OF A KING
A bomb blast at the signing of the Sokovia Accords in Vienna claims the life of King T'Chaka of Wakanda. This alters Prince T'Challa's motivation from seeking justice for those killed in Lagos, to a personal yearning for retribution.

DEFYING ORDERS
Captain America is told to either sign the Accords or retire, but he isn't willing to do either. After his friend Bucky Barnes, a.k.a. the Winter Soldier, is implicated in the Vienna bombing, Cap's ally in the CIA, Sharon Carter, notifies him of Bucky's location. Black Widow warns Cap to stay out of it and let the task force retrieve Bucky, but Cap won't let his childhood friend get killed. He places his loyalty to Bucky above his duties as an Avenger, and his own reputation.

In Germany, Captain America pursues Black Panther, who himself is chasing the Winter Soldier. Cap's intention was to find his friend before the authorities did and quietly sneak him to safety, but German Special Forces and the CIA intervene, leading to a wild and destructive chase through the city traffic.

HELMUT ZEMO
Seeking revenge for the death of his family in Sokovia, the former colonel Helmut Zemo laid the bomb in Vienna as part of a plot to destroy the Avengers. Once Zemo has the Winter Soldier codebook, his next step is to reactivate Bucky's Winter Soldier programming.

German Special Forces (KSK) commando

Winter Soldier pinned to ground

Captain America's arms and hands immobilized

CIVIL WAR

The Avengers' internal conflict is a fight that nobody really wants. Captain America believes his friend Bucky Barnes is innocent of the terrorist acts he is accused of, and is committed to protecting him. Everyone on Cap's side is also opposed to the restrictive Sokovia Accords, wanting to maintain their personal liberty. On the other side, Tony Stark is driven by guilt over the collateral damage caused by the Avengers in Sokovia. Vision believes in maintaining order, while War Machine is more legalistic about it all. Unknowingly, all have fallen into a trap set for them by a vengeful Sokovian named Helmut Zemo.

After Bucky is captured, Tony Stark and Captain America rehash the situation at Everett K. Ross' Joint Terrorism Task Force Center in Berlin. At this point, Stark is still amiable, but frustrated with Cap's stubborn refusal to go along with the Accords.

BATTLE LINES

Both sides in the Avengers Civil War are relatively evenly matched, which makes it hard for either to gain the upper hand. Both sides also have secret weapons: "Giant-Man" for Cap, and Spider-Man for Stark.

TEAM CAP

Falcon
Ant-Man ("Giant-Man")
Hawkeye
Scarlet Witch
Captain America
Winter Soldier

TEAM STARK

Iron Man
Black Panther
Vision
Black Widow
Spider-Man
War Machine

Shield snatched from Captain America

Eye pieces filter stimuli

Parker has grown up hearing tales of the Avengers' heroism, and finds himself in the unusual situation of having to fight his own childhood heroes. Caught off guard by Parker's questions, Falcon tells him that in most fights "there isn't this much talking."

SPIDER-MAN

Tony Stark needs an edge in the looming fight with Cap. Young Peter Parker's unusual agility, reflexes, and knack for web-slinging have caught Stark's attention. He recruits Parker—a.k.a. Spider-Man—and equips him with cutting-edge tech. Parker is meant to stay on the periphery, but Spider-Man's youthful enthusiasm causes him to swing into the center of the action.

Spider symbol is a detachable drone

Suit created by Stark Industries

Utility belt holds web fluid cartridges

Sleek material minimizes drag

Cap has fought alongside the Avengers on Stark's team many times, and knows their relative strengths and weaknesses. Spider-Man's sudden appearance and unusual skills catch him off balance, literally.

Captain America's team arrives at Leipzig-Halle Airport, in search of a Quinjet that Cap and Barnes will use to fly to an old Hydra facility in Siberia. There, they will prevent Helmut Zemo from awakening other Winter Soldiers held in stasis, and ultimately clear Bucky's name. Stark's side is obliged to stop them, aware that failure to do so will make the authorities come down harder on everyone. The resulting battle causes millions of dollars' worth of damage.

DATA FILE

> Hydra's secret Siberian Winter Soldier training facility was run by Colonel Vasily Karpov of the Russian Armed Forces.

> Zemo never intended to wake the Winter Soldiers; he merely used them as bait to lure the Avengers.

TONY'S REVENGE

Once Tony realizes that the Winter Soldier murdered his parents, Barnes' innocence in the Vienna bombing no longer matters to him. Capturing Bucky is out of the question—Tony means to kill him.

SIBERIAN ENDGAME

Realizing Bucky's innocence, Iron Man joins Cap and the Winter Soldier in the abandoned Hydra facility in Siberia. Here, Zemo reveals the real reason for his deception—he shows them a tape of Barnes, as the Winter Soldier, murdering Tony Stark's parents in 1991. Zemo's aim was never to fight the Avengers himself, but rather to get them to fight each other. Stark becomes enraged and the battle between him and Captain America leaves their friendship, and the Avengers, in ruins.

Unibeam charging up

Their battle leaves both Cap and Iron Man without their primary weapons. Stark's Mark XLVI armor is damaged beyond repair, while Cap abandons his shield after Tony tells him that it really belongs to his father, Howard Stark.

Bucky's cybernetic arm is no match for Iron Man's Unibeam

Water expelled from tanks for buoyancy

Landing bay hatch

THE RAFT

The Raft is a submersible vessel in a secret location in the Atlantic Ocean. It is the most secure prison on the planet—perfect for holding enhanced individuals. After capture, most of Cap's team are held in cellblock R1. Wanda Maximoff is kept in isolation in cell NZ42.

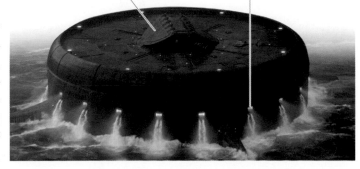

IRON MAN

Businessman Tony Stark is possibly the last person anyone expects to become a Super Hero, including himself. Content to live the lifestyle that his multi-billion-dollar fortune affords him, Stark rarely considers the difficulties of those less fortunate. But then a life-changing event sets him on a path he never dreamed of, transforming him into one of Earth's most powerful weapons: a flying armored warrior, virtually invulnerable and peerless in battle, famous around the world simply as "Iron Man."

"SOMETIMES YOU GOTTA RUN BEFORE YOU CAN WALK."

TONY STARK

TONY STARK

Anthony Edward Stark is a gifted engineer with a sarcastic sense of humor, who astutely self-identifies as a "genius, billionaire, playboy, philanthropist." When his parents, Howard and Maria Stark, were killed, young Stark took over the family business and grew it into one of the most successful tech companies in the world. His greatest invention, the Iron Man armor, catches the attention of S.H.I.E.L.D. and Stark is asked to join the Avengers.

Core made from salvaged palladium

PROOF THAT TONY STARK HAS A HEART

MARK I MINI ARC REACTOR

A business trip to Afghanistan changes Stark's life forever. His heart is grievously wounded in a terrorist ambush, forcing him to develop a new technology to keep himself alive. This miniaturized Arc Reactor, also known as a Repulsor Tech node (RT) becomes the key to powering his Iron Man suits.

Inscription from Pepper Potts

Hair groomed by in-house Stark Industries stylist

Cables link to reactor in Tony's chest

BILLIONAIRE GENIUS

Following in his father's footsteps, Tony Stark's skills with technology are almost without equal. He graduated from MIT at the age of 17 with a B.S. in engineering, and inherited his father's company, Stark Industries, at age 21, making him the youngest-ever CEO of a Fortune 500 company. Under his direction, Stark Industries grew to a net worth of $120 billion and Stark himself amassed a $75.43 billion fortune. Much of this wealth came from the sale of highly destructive weapon systems.

Shirt and tie selected by Pepper Potts

David August single-breasted suit with notched lapel

MARK III SUIT REPULSOR TEST

TRIAL AND ERROR

After the first prototype armor he builds with fellow prisoner Dr. Ho Yinsen in Afghanistan, Tony Stark creates his other Iron Man suits alone in his private workshop. He tests them all himself, which means lots of crashes, contusions, and black eyes.

Mark II prototype

Crushed Shelby Cobra 427

Tony Stark is a self-confessed adrenaline junkie and racing enthusiast. He has a large car collection, and his company sponsors drivers around the world. On a visit to Europe he drives a 1978 Wolf Ford replica in the Grand Prix de Monaco Historique.

Compression shirt improves blood flow to muscles

Advanced RT

A CHANGED MAN

Stark's experiences as a hostage in Afghanistan—seeing his company's weapons being used by terrorists—change his entire world view. He resolves to no longer develop and sell advanced weapons indiscriminately. As the hero Iron Man, his new focus is on clearing up past mistakes and eliminating threats around the world.

Stark plays a vital role in the Super Hero team known as the Avengers. He is their primary source of funding and advanced technology, and alongside Captain America, helps develop their battle strategies.

Pepper Potts begins as Tony Stark's personal assistant before jumping to the top position in his company. She has always been irreplaceable to Tony—nobody else would put up with his danger-seeking, erratic behavior. Before long, they fall in love.

Mark XLII suit damaged in Killian's attack on Stark's home

Shrapnel still in chest

FACING HIS DEMONS

Although his outlook has changed, sometimes Tony's past comes back to haunt him. His rude dismissal of fellow engineer Aldrich Killian back in 1999 set Killian on a path of revenge and murder.

Bespoke sneakers made to Tony's own specifications

DATA FILE

> After defeating Aldrich Killian, Stark finally has the remaining shrapnel removed from his heart by Dr. Wu, who was originally introduced to Stark by Dr. Ho Yinsen in 1999.

> Tony Stark uses the shrapnel removed from his chest to make a necklace for Pepper.

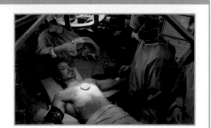

IRON MAN

Tony Stark's Iron Man armors are more than just protective metal suits—these unrivaled feats of engineering transform him into a flying warrior, powered by a unique renewable energy source and armed with state-of-the-art weaponry. Iron Man is Stark's crowning achievement, and the ultimate weapon to protect Earth from terrorist groups, extraterrestrial invasions, or supernatural threats.

Repulsors are the key technology that makes Tony's suits possible. They convert the raw power of his Arc Reactor/Repulsor Tech node (RT) into directed streams of energy, which he can then use for propulsion, or as weapons.

Iron Man's user interface is called JARVIS. This artificial intelligence system highlights threats, provides system status updates and damage reports, and identifies potential strategies and enemy weaknesses. When JARVIS is used to form Vision's consciousness, Stark creates a new, female A.I. known as FRIDAY.

Next-generation repulsor

Tactile sensors built into fingers aid grip

RT with powerful Unibeam blast

Six missile launchers on each shoulder

Auditory Dissonance Apraxia Module

Visual sensors linked to FRIDAY augmented reality (AR) displays

Entire helmet retracts into collar

Rocket launcher and lasers on each wrist

MARK XLVI ARMOR

Worn during the Avengers' own civil war, Iron Man's 46th iteration features the FRIDAY A.I. interface (first adopted in the Mark XLV to replace JARVIS). The suit's other innovations include a fully collapsible helmet, enhanced strength and damage resistance, and rapid-charge repulsors.

Streamlined components maximize flying speed

Iron Man's armors are capable of flying rapidly to almost any location on the planet. Late models can reach hypersonic speeds (beyond Mach 5).

Ankle shock absorbers

FRONT VIEW

PRIMARY WEAPON

Iron Man's Unibeam is his most powerful weapon. The main RT in the center of his chest powers a special repulsor that fires a concentrated blast of energy. This beam is powerful enough to vaporize metal.

Upgraded auxiliary thrusters

Reinforced knee plates

High-impact shock-absorbers

Impact sensors built into surface plates

95.5 percent titanium, 4.5 percent gold alloy plating

Auxiliary repulsors allows separate components to fly

Newbold M3 abdominal servos

POWERED UP

Stark's earlier armors are powered by the RT in his chest. Later suits incorporate their own independent reactors, while the most recent models, like the Mark XLVI, have secondary back-up reactors built throughout.

SIDE VIEW

DOCTOR HO YINSEN

Dr. Ho Yinsen is a world-renowned surgeon from the little village of Gulmira in Afghanistan. Despite meeting Tony Stark at a New Year's Eve party in Bern, Switzerland, in 1999, Stark doesn't remember Yinsen years later when they are both held captive by the terrorist organization, The Ten Rings. Yinsen saves Stark's life by operating on a bomb wound to his heart and installs a powerful electromagnet in Stark's chest to keep the remaining shrapnel from killing him. Yinsen's kindness and urging to seek a better path inspire Stark to change his ways and become the hero known as Iron Man.

KIND-HEARTED STRANGER

Yinsen is a good man who has every reason to be bitter—his family were murdered by The Ten Rings. Instead, he channels his grief into positive actions, and his purpose now is to make the most of his feeble situation and try to thwart the terrorists. Yinsen teaches Stark how to survive in the terrorist camp by pretending to comply with The Ten Rings' demands. All the while, Yinsen assists Stark in his escape plan, knowing he will never be able to leave himself. Yinsen saves Tony Stark's life twice, and ultimately sacrifices himself so Stark can live.

Yinsen always wears tie, even in captivity

Tools for electronics work

Eyeglasses from Singapore

Magnifying lens for precise work

Yinsen assists Tony Stark in building his prototype miniature Arc Reactor/Repulsor Tech node (RT) in their prison-cave laboratory. The palladium-core reactor will produce three gigajoules of power—enough to power Stark's heart for 50 lifetimes.

The Ten Rings' leader Raza Al-Wazar grows suspicious that Stark and Yinsen are working on something other than the missile he asked for. He visits their workshop and threatens to maim Yinsen, but Tony saves him by insisting he needs Yinsen as his assistant.

Raza gives Stark and Yinsen only one more day to complete a missile, so the pair work feverishly overnight to finish Stark's Mark I suit instead. Yinsen realizes they don't have enough time, and sacrifices himself to buy Tony a few more minutes.

DATA FILE

> Yinsen speaks many languages, including English, Arabic, Russian, French, and a few phrases in Hungarian.

> Yinsen's steady hands make him a very capable surgeon, and are vital for assembling the Mark I's jury-rigged components.

Melted palladium ready for mold

THE TEN RINGS

With a global reach, The Ten Rings is one of the world's most prominent and dangerous terrorist organizations. Its cells spread across every continent, specializing in kidnap, extortion, and attacks on civilians. Tony Stark first encounters them when he is kidnapped in Afghanistan on a business trip. Even after Stark cuts off their supply of deadly weapons, The Ten Rings remains a global threat. Most recently, they attempted to acquire militarized Yellowjacket suits from Pym Tech's CEO, Darren Cross.

As prisoners, Tony Stark and Ho Yinsen have little else to do when they take breaks so they drink tea, play backgammon, and chat about their lives. Raza has no desire to deal with his prisoners directly, unless absolutely necessary, so he sends his dim-witted proxy, Abu Bakaar.

Decorative strip may include coded message

Swords symbol warns that enemies will be cut down

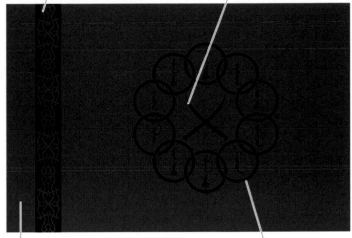

FLAG OF THE TEN RINGS

Blood-red background color

Circles represent ten power rings worn by the group's founder

Raza's men recover Tony Stark's wrecked Mark I armor from the desert and bring it back to camp. They lack the engineering skills needed to repair it, so Raza decides to use it as a bargaining chip.

RAZA AL-WAZAR

Raza Hamidmi Al-Wazar is the leader of the Ten Rings cell that kidnaps Stark. Well-educated and fluent in English, Raza is also cruel and is not above using torture. Raza's overconfidence allows Stark to build the Iron Man prototype instead of advanced missiles under Raza's own nose and escape, while his arrogance in trying to renegotiate his deal with Stark's corrupt business partner, Obadiah Stane, ultimately gets him killed.

Traditional scarf keeps out cold of Afghanistan's mountains

Stolen British army disruptive pattern material (DPM)

Hot coal intended for use as torture implement

V-Bit blacksmith tongs

STARK'S HOUSE AND WORKSHOP

For many years, Tony Stark lives at 10880 Malibu Point, in Malibu, California. His fortune affords him an impressively sized mansion in one of the priciest spots in the U.S., conveniently situated close to the Californian tech industry and celebrity party life. His lifestyle is that of a solitary bachelor until Pepper Potts moves in with him, though his driver Happy Hogan occasionally stays. The home is eventually destroyed by Stark's business rival Aldrich Killian, and Tony moves to Stark (later Avengers) Tower in Manhattan.

Mâcon white wine

$300 bottle of Napa Valley Cabernet Sauvignon

Tony Stark has an enviable wine collection with only the best local Californian Cabernet Sauvignon vintages, as well as white wine from Mâcon, France.

Stark's piano overlooks a spacious lounge with a fireplace and waterfall. Stairs lead down to the workshop.

1949 Mercury Coupe

1932 Ford Model B Roadster

Personalized license plate

STARK11

THE STARK ESTATE

Tony Stark's mansion rests on a cliff overlooking the Pacific Ocean. He has everything a billionaire could want—multiple bedrooms, offices, a games room, and lots of space for entertaining. The estate is fully integrated with his A.I. system JARVIS and conveniently located near his company HQ in Los Angeles.

CAR COLLECTION

Tony has a lot of disposable income and invests a substantial portion into cars. His tastes run the gamut, from vintage automobiles through milestones of innovation and style, to flashy new trendsetters. His workshop and garage adjoin, which results in some unfortunate mishaps.

Helicopter landing pad

Entryway with spiral staircases and seating area

Entertaining area with seating and bar

HIGH-TECH WORKSHOP

Tony has a private workshop in his basement where he builds all of his Iron Man armors. There, he has few distractions and can work out of sight of any agents of corporate espionage. His equipment is state of the art and is constantly upgraded, allowing him to rapidly produce new Iron Man iterations. Underneath the main workshop is a bunker, where most of Tony's Iron Man models are stored, along with other valuables. Tony's servers are stored in his workshop, with backups located in the bunker.

LAB DISPLAYS

Countless screens cover every surface in the workshop. They show close-ups of Iron Man component schematics and performance gauges.

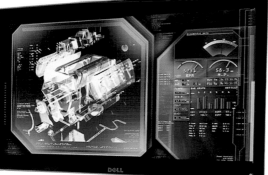

Finely tuned diagnostic computer

Computer monitor displays blueprints

Widescreen television monitor tracks power levels

Rack-mounted servers

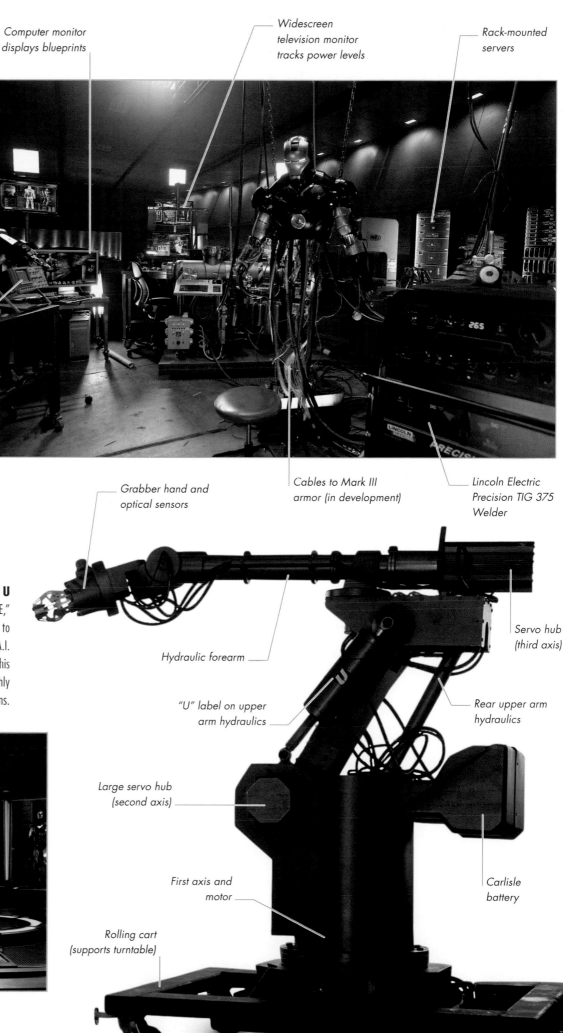

Grabber hand and optical sensors

Cables to Mark III armor (in development)

Lincoln Electric Precision TIG 375 Welder

Hydraulic forearm

Servo hub (third axis)

"U" label on upper arm hydraulics

Rear upper arm hydraulics

Large servo hub (second axis)

First axis and motor

Carlisle battery

Rolling cart (supports turntable)

DUM-E AND U

Tony Stark built the first of his two workshop robots, "Dum-E," when he was a 16-year-old student at MIT and later went on to construct "U." The two robotic arms are equipped with an A.I. that responds to Stark's voice commands and learns from his behavior. Despite their basic appearance, they are highly intelligent and versatile—they can even exhibit emotions.

Tony Stark keeps the Mark I through Mark VII suits on display in his "Hall of Armor" at one end of his workshop. He addresses them as "ladies" while testing the Mark XLII.

IRON MAN SUITS

Tony Stark's first prototype Iron Man armor (the Mark I) is built under extreme duress while a prisoner of The Ten Rings. Its sole purpose is to help him escape. When he returns home, Stark is inspired to continue developing his Iron Man suits, using them to combat terrorists who are using his company's weapons around the globe. The Mark II to Mark VII armors are built in his workshop at his Malibu mansion. Each offers incremental improvements over the one before it. All seven are displayed in a gallery in Stark's workshop, and are destroyed when Stark's home is blown up by his rival, Aldrich Killian.

Arc Reactor/
Repulsor Tech
node (RT)

Flamethrower
tank

MARK I
This jury-rigged prototype suit fuses onboard computers from a guided missile and ballistic missile. It is armed with flamethrowers and single-use jet thrusters.

Hydraulic
legs carry
1,500 lbs
(680 kg) suit

Servo-powered
arms can lift
900 lbs
(408 kg)

MARK II
The first suit created by Tony Stark at home, the Mark II is also the first to have repulsor flight stabilizers and a JARVIS A.I. upload. It later becomes the first War Machine armor.

MARK III
The first iconic red-and-yellow suit, the Mark III's outer hull is weaker than the Mark II, but easily flies at high altitudes. It is the first equipped with a Unibeam weapon.

Unibeam
over RT

Air brakes
(slow suit from Mach
2 in only 5 seconds)

Damage from
battle with
Obadiah Stane

Repulsors in
feet modules

Smart
targeting
computer
linked to
missiles

Unpainted
hull ices up at
high altitudes

Armor-piercing
rocket mounted
in each arm

Supersonic thrust
boots capable of
1,500 mph
(2,414 kph)

MARK IV
The Mark IV upgrades the Mark III's external Unibeam with a thermoplastic lens, adding a prismatic shutter to focus the beam's light energy.

MARK V
This suit compresses into a 33 lbs (15 kg) suitcase for easy transport. Its biometric security system scans retinas, face, fingerprints, voice, and brainwaves to prevent theft.

Gold
titanium
exoskeleton

Segmented
plates collapse
into smaller size

Satellite phone
with excellent
reception

Triangular
Unibeam lens
is unique

Laser system

MARK VI
The Mark VI is developed to use the higher power output of Stark's upgraded RT, which is fueled by a new element. It includes prototype lasers in the back of each gauntlet, as well as advanced micro-munition missile launchers.

Shoulder-
deployed smart
micro missiles

MARK VII
First deployed during the Battle of New York, this suit activates remotely and is coded to home in on bracelets worn by Tony Stark.

Additional auxiliary
thrusters

NEXT-GENERATION ARMORS

Stark's newest armors can assemble onto his body by matching to computer chips implanted under his skin. Individual pieces can fly autonomously, thanks to mini-repulsors throughout the armor, and most of the suits can be used as drones. Some of them can also form around other people on Stark's voice commands. Stark gives some of the more specialist "Iron Legion" armors nicknames, including "Heartbreaker" (Mark XVII, artillery), "Striker" (Mark XXV, heavy construction), and "Igor" (Mark XXXVIII, heavy lifting).

MARK XLII

This suit can operate autonomously as a sentry, or be controlled remotely via a headset. This causes tension between Tony and Pepper when he uses it as a proxy to interact with her. Its security protocols prove much too aggressive.

Right arm worn by Pepper to dispatch Aldrich Killian

Magnetized feet for walking upside down

Individual pieces keyed to chips in Stark's skin

MARK XLIV: THE "HULKBUSTER"

The Mark XLIV is a unique addition to Stark's armory. It is a massive exoskeleton that encases one of Stark's standard suits, giving him vastly increased strength and durability at the cost of mobility. This makes it ideal for emergency Hulk-containment operations.

Extra layers of armor in helmet protect Stark from Hulk punches

Suit's pieces deployed from orbiting satellite

Infra-red scanner sees through walls

Repulsor can blast through 3 ft (0.9 m) of concrete

Hydraulic rams can deliver powerful blows

Legs must bear suit's enormous weight, hindering maneuverability

MARK XLIII

This highly-weaponized suit is worn during the war against Hydra in Sokovia. It includes upgraded repulsors, shoulder-mounted cannons, anti-armor tank missiles fired from the gauntlets, and fortress-infiltrator missiles.

PEPPER POTTS

Virginia "Pepper" Potts is Tony Stark's highly capable personal assistant. She often handles damage control to the reputations of both Stark and his company, following Iron Man's more chaotic adventures, and is exasperated by his careless attitude. Stark promotes Potts as Stark Industries' new CEO, a move that he had already been pondering for some time, but is hastened by his belief that he is dying. Their professional relationship soon turns romantic, making Pepper a target for Stark's foes when she is kidnapped by a business rival and nearly killed. Despite this, and other bumps in the road, her loyalty to Tony never wavers.

Stark courts so much danger that at times Potts must become a Super Hero herself. Tony teaches Pepper the Iron Man basics, so that in an emergency she can use his Mark XLII suit.

Pepper's outfit reflects keen, professional fashion sense

SAVING TONY STARK

Stark would never survive without Pepper. On at least two occasions she personally defeats Tony's antagonists and saves his life. First she destroys Obadiah Stane and his Iron Monger armor with a well-timed blast from a giant Arc Reactor. Then, after surviving a fiery fall thanks to her body being infused with Extremis, Pepper kills the terrorist Aldrich Killian. She plays a continuous role in saving Tony from life-threatening situations, whether directly, or from behind the scenes. Sometimes, it is even a matter of saving Tony from himself.

Pepper is Tony's emotional anchor. She knows that events during the Chitauri invasion of Earth are weighing on his mind, and worries when she finds Tony tinkering in his workshop, instead of being with her.

STARK INDUSTRIES CEO

Pepper is far more business-focused than Tony ever was. Yet much of her time as CEO is spent cleaning up Tony's messes—like reclaiming the Mark II prototype—which distracts her from her duties of actually running the company.

Belt from a trendy Malibu boutique

Ring was a gift from Pepper's grandmother

HAPPY HOGAN

Harold "Happy" Hogan is the closest and most trusted friend of Tony Stark and Pepper Potts. His nickname pokes fun at his typically grim demeanor, though he has a big heart. Happy serves as Stark's bodyguard and driver for many years, and is promoted to Head of Security for Stark Industries by Potts. He is nearly killed in an explosion credited to the terrorist known as the Mandarin, though Aldrich Killian is really responsible. Happy recovers and continues working for Stark Industries, also serving as an unofficial assistant and right-hand man to Stark.

Eyes watch for suspicious people and other threats

Perfectly knotted tie

Happy begins his employment with Stark as his chauffeur and is later promoted to bodyguard. He accompanies his boss and keeps an eye out for his well-being. He also screens Stark's prospective dates.

Heavy-set, but strong and in shape

As Head of Security, Happy is wary of anyone who looks suspicious, and develops something akin to a sixth sense for danger. He follows Aldrich Killian's henchman, Eric Savin, stopping him at the Chinese Theatre in Hollywood, just before a huge explosion.

BODYGUARD AND FRIEND

Happy is an excellent driver and has access to Tony's impressive car collection, including a 1932 Flathead Roadster and 1967 Shelby Cobra. He has fighting skills to back up his bodyguard role, too. Happy is an amateur boxer and often spars with Tony. He dutifully puts Pepper and Tony's lives before his own. Tony may tease Happy, but he appreciates his friend's loyalty and is devastated when Happy is seriously injured by a terrorist explosion.

Iron Man Mark V briefcase—the "football"—weighs 33lbs (15kg)

Happy takes initiative, always proving himself to Tony and Pepper. He doesn't hesitate to jump into action—speeding off to stop the criminal engineer Ivan Vanko and his ally, Justin Hammer.

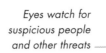

WAR MACHINE

Colonel James "Rhodey" Rhodes (code name: War Machine) is a U.S. Air Force pilot and best friend of Tony Stark. Rhodes is an honorable soldier who often struggles to reconcile his duty to the military and his loyalty to his reckless friend. Fortunately, Stark's problems often align with issues of national security. Suited in his armor, Rhodes assists Stark against sinister schemes by Ivan Vanko, Aldrich Killian, and the android Ultron. After he joins the Avengers, Rhodey is once again torn between duty and friendship when half of the team refuses to sign the restrictive Sokovia Accords.

M134 Minigun

DATA FILE

> War Machine's shoulder-mounted cannon has several nicknames including "Torso Taker" and "Powder Maker." Its high rate of fire means it requires a 9,000 round ammunition supply.

> Rhodes has flown 138 combat missions with the U.S. Air Force.

WAR MACHINE (MARK I)

The War Machine Mark I suit is actually the Iron Man Mark II armor. Rhodes confiscates it from an intoxicated Stark who is behaving dangerously at his own birthday party. Rhodes hands the armor to the U.S. Air Force, but is distressed to learn they have contracted Stark's rival, Justin Hammer, to upgrade the suit, rebranding it War Machine. The armor gets a few aesthetic changes, but most of the added weaponry is sub-par and fails to work correctly in battle.

Rhodes serves as a liaison between the U.S. military and Stark Industries. His military work ethic and Stark's irresponsible playboy lifestyle can cause the friends to clash at times.

Aileron (hinged surface) for added flight control

Iron Man and War Machine team up to fight off Justin Hammer's military drones, but all of Rhodey's suit upgrades malfunction.

Thruster boots calibrated by onboard computer

Cannon mounted on articulated arm

"FF" stands for 1st Fighter Wing

IRON PATRIOT (MARK II)

Tony Stark builds a new suit for his friend so he can reclaim the Iron Man Mark II for himself. Rhodes now has a reliable armor of his own, without any of Justin Hammer's faulty technology. The U.S. government once again orders Rhodes to have his suit upgraded, though; this time by Aldrich Killian's Advanced Idea Mechanics (AIM). The upgrade includes a new paint job and rebranding as "Iron Patriot."

The government can't control Tony Stark and his Iron Man suit, so they settle for the next best thing: Iron Patriot. Nonetheless, Rhodes still makes himself available to help his friend.

Rhodey also wears the Mark II suit, long-since stripped of its patriotic color scheme, against the rogue android Ultron in Sokovia.

WAR MACHINE (MARK III)

Tony Stark creates a third iteration of the War Machine armor for Rhodes after the Battle of Sokovia. The Mark III is highly weaponized, with two machine guns mounted on each forearm, missile launchers on each shoulder, and a sonic cannon installed in the back of the right hand. Rhodes wears the armor during the Avengers' internal conflict, where it is severely damaged.

HUD powered by multi-processor computer system with GPS and target scanning

Dual-barreled shoulder cannon fires 6,000 rounds per minute

The armor's repulsor thrusters are strong enough to carry passengers. Spider-Man catches a ride with War Machine during the Avengers' skirmish at Leipzig-Halle Airport.

Third-generation weapons-grade repulsor flight stabilizers

Rhodes argues in favor of signing the Sokovia Accords during the Avengers' discussions. His military background leads him to agree that the team needs to adhere to international law and be held accountable for its actions. His beliefs align him with Tony Stark, but pit him against Captain America and Falcon.

Ultron sentry kill markings

Wrist-mounted assault rifle

Hull pressure transducers automatically adjust to environment

Compact retractable machine guns stored on hips

Rhodes is accidentally hit by a blast from fellow Avenger Vision during the airport battle. Though both Falcon and Iron Man try to catch him, neither are fast enough to reach Rhodes, who falls uncontrollably to the ground. His spine is shattered from his L4 through S1 vertebrae.

Chromed titanium and steel exoskeleton

Baton head pulls upward to reveal stun panels

Four stun panels can be set to various strengths

STUN BATON

War Machine wields a "War Hammer" stun baton to avoid seriously injuring his colleagues during the Avengers' Civil War. The non-lethal weapon is stored in a recessed charger in the back of his armor.

Shock pulse emitted if kick makes contact with opponent

OBADIAH STANE

Tony Stark's business partner, Obadiah Stane, projects a benevolent persona, but in reality he is both cold hearted and treacherous. A close friend of Tony's father, Howard, he stepped in as interim CEO of Stark Industries when Howard and his wife were killed in 1991. Tony Stark took over the company aged 21, and Stane became his second-in-command and mentor. Secretly, he is jealous and resentful of Stark, and hires the terrorist group The Ten Rings to kill him. Unfortunately for Stane, Stark creates the first Iron Man armor and escapes from captivity. Stane copies the design and builds his own "Iron Monger" suit, his toxic ambition leading to a final, fatal confrontation.

Frown lines and grimace hint at bitterness

Stark wants his company to pursue Arc Reactor technology instead of weapons. When Stane reminds him that they haven't had a reactor breakthrough in 30 years, Stark shows him the new miniaturized Arc Reactor in his chest—but wisely refuses to share the tech with Stane.

Obadiah Stane enjoys the limelight almost as much as Stark does. He takes great pride in appearing on the covers of magazines and is jealous when young Tony receives such accolades, after he himself has put so much more time into the company. When Obadiah throws a company party he doesn't even invite Stark, though he shows up anyway.

Stane routinely accepts awards on Stark's behalf, while the billionaire playboy is out living the highlife.

BUSINESS "PARTNER"

Obadiah Stane started out working at Howard Stark's munitions company, Stark International, after World War II. He assisted Howard (and Anton Vanko) in creating the original Arc Reactor, but the prototype proved too expensive to develop further. Since Tony took over the Stark legacy, Stane has acted as his adviser, but behind the scenes has been aggressively working against him. He views Stark as a threat, stealing whatever ideas Stark produces while also marginalizing him.

Pockets hide sonic stun device

Suspicious of Stane's motives, Stark's assistant, Pepper, searches Stane's computer and discovers schematics for the Iron Monger suit as well as secret manifests for missile shipments to Pakistan and Afghanistan. The most shocking item is a video from The Ten Rings, proving Stane himself hired them to kill Stark.

Tailored suit cost $4,500

Shoes covered in Afghan dust

DATA FILE

> Stane carries a prototype sonic stun device that he originally developed for the military. He uses it to paralyze Stark.

> Stane is an accomplished amateur pianist.

> The sprawling Stark Industries campus is so extensive that Stane rides a Segway from place to place.

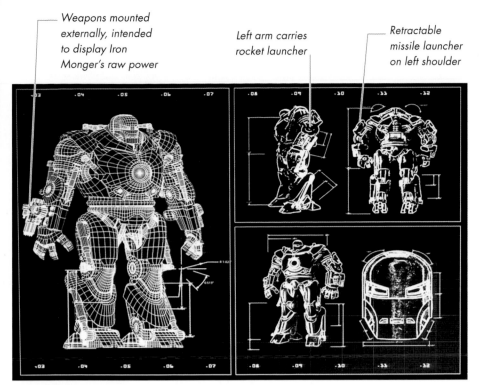

Weapons mounted externally, intended to display Iron Monger's raw power

Left arm carries rocket launcher

Retractable missile launcher on left shoulder

Stane has a secret laboratory in Sector-16, located in the basement of Stark Industries' headquarters, just below the old full-sized Arc Reactor prototype. His overworked engineers attempt to improve upon Stark's Iron Man design, but struggle to recreate its propulsion systems and power supply.

IRON MONGER ARMOR

The Iron Monger suit has minimal navigational systems; it focuses on smart weapons and targeting sensors instead. Primary weapons include S-category missiles and a gatling cannon mounted on the right wrist. The suit does not function reliably at low temperatures and pressures, however, as its systems freeze solid.

THE IRON MONGER

Obadiah Stane believes that manufacturing weapons is the only way Stark Industries can succeed. Seeing the potential of Tony's Mark I prototype, he steals its broken remains from The Ten Rings and uses it to build his own, larger suit of armor. His design incorporates powerful limbs controlled by massive servo-hydraulics, with a hull made from proprietary Omnium steel. When Pepper and Tony discover Stane's sinister plans, he dons the armor and attacks them. Stane is killed in the ensuing battle with Iron Man, though S.H.I.E.L.D. covers up the details of his death, saying he died in a plane crash while on vacation.

Arms can hurl objects up to 15,000 lbs (6,804 kg) in weight

Shoulder and head swivel up to access gyroscopic body harness

Chamber holds RT stolen from Tony Stark's chest

JUSTIN HAMMER

Hammer Industries CEO, Justin Hammer, is Tony Stark's sleaziest rival. He is also largely incompetent—Hammer confidently boasts of his achievements, but when it comes to actually producing anything, he usually steals other people's intellectual property. His schemes tend to backfire. When he forces Stark's nemesis, Ivan Vanko, into duplicating Stark's tech, Vanko double-crosses him, leaving Hammer helpless, humiliated, and on his way to prison.

Hammer tries to impress journalist Christine Everhart by suggesting he and Tony Stark are good friends.

Showy tie

Single-breasted 3-piece suit with notched lapel

Stinger missiles

Wrist-mounted machine gun and guided missile launcher

Vanko-designed Arc Reactor

HAMMER DRONES

Using Ivan Vanko's engineering genius, Justin Hammer develops drones for the U.S. Army, Navy, Air Force, and Marines. Each branch of the military has a unique set of customizations, such as grenade launchers, thermal vision, and tank guns.

Vanko secretly programs the drones so he can seize control of them at the Hammer Expo and use them to destroy Iron Man.

Chobham armor

NAVY DRONE

CORRUPT CEO

Justin Hammer only gets ahead by stealing other people's work. His own efforts to replicate Stark's Iron Man armor fail miserably, so Hammer attempts to discredit Stark and gain his technology through sleazy government intervention. When this also fails, he forcefully recruits Ivan Vanko to build similar armored suits—though Vanko has his own agenda and builds drones instead. He gains access to the Iron Man Mark II armor after Lt. Col. Rhodes confiscates it, and upgrades it to create the first—highly defective—War Machine armor.

M134 Minigun

Extravagantly expensive shoes

Hammer's corrupt political ally, Senator Stern, calls Rhodes to testify against Tony Stark—trying to discredit Stark and award his Iron Man tech to Hammer—but the effort backfires.

WHIPLASH

Ivan Antonovich Vanko is a Russian engineer and physicist with a painful past. He spent 15 years in prison for trying to sell plutonium to Pakistan, and his father endured a similar fate for attempting to sell Arc Reactor technology to terrorists. Believing that the Starks stole his father's legacy, Ivan builds his own reactor and a powered suit with lethal electro-whips. Vanko is captured when he attacks Stark and gets sent to prison, giving Justin Hammer an opportunity to outdo his business rival. He fakes Vanko's death and forces Vanko to make weapons for him.

DATA FILE

> Vanko's crude first suit, the Mark I, focuses the repulsor technology through ionized plasma channels.

> Whiplash's Mark II suit combines a stronger version of his electro-whips with a full-bodied metal suit that increases his strength and is capable of flight.

> Vanko uses a fake I.D. to get into the Monaco Grand Prix, which identifies him as Boris Turgenov.

Straggly, unkempt hair

THIRST FOR REVENGE

Ivan Vanko's father Anton co-invented the Arc Reactor with Howard Stark (father of Tony). When Anton tried to sell it behind Stark's back, he was deported and ended up in a Russian gulag. Following Anton's death, Ivan obsesses about revenge. He says he wants to show the entire world that a Stark can be beaten, and chooses the very public arena of the Monaco Grand Prix to launch his first vicious attack on Tony Stark.

After his father passes away, Ivan Vanko bitterly goes to work in his grimy Moscow home. He creates an Arc Reactor based on tech developed by his father, and a weaponized harness.

Vanko does not fear Lt. Col. Rhodes' War Machine armor as he believes the suit is under his control. Moreover, its Hammer Industries upgrades are ineffective.

Leather harness attaches technology to upper body

Russian prison tattoos

Metal exoskeleton

VANKO'S PARROT

Lonely Vanko's only friend is his parrot. When he is "hired" by Hammer, Vanko demands that Hammer retrieve his parrot from Russia. However, Hammer gives him a different bird.

External mini Arc Reactor

White cockatoo

Tinted sunglasses

ALDRICH KILLIAN

Smooth-talking, charismatic Aldrich Killian is a scientist, entrepreneur, and founder of a think tank named AIM (Advanced Idea Mechanics). Once scorned by Tony Stark, Killian has seen his life turn around thanks to the powers of a technology called Extremis. Not only is he now imbued with incredible self-healing and heat-generating powers, but he even boasts the alarming capacity to breathe fire. Underneath his charming exterior lies a maniac with an ambitious plan to manipulate the war on terrorism from both sides, scoring huge profits for his company.

Impeccably groomed hair

Mouth twisted into slight smirk

Hoping for Stark Industries' investment, Aldrich's slick holographic presentation with a live feed from his own brain astonishes CEO Pepper Potts. His pitch showcases Extremis' ability to recode a human body's DNA for healing.

Pricey rings indicative of financial success

Pepper is flustered by Killian's changed appearance and self-assured behavior. Despite the fact that she will not invest in his project, as it could be weaponized too easily, he seems to bear her no ill feelings.

A NEW MAN

Killian first met Tony Stark in 1999, during a New Year's Eve party at a science conference in Bern, Switzerland. His socially awkward behavior and physical disabilities led Tony to scoff at Killian's enthusiasm for his new, privately funded think tank. More than a decade later, Killian is now a healthy, wealthy success story. Extremis' biogenetic enhancements have helped him achieve maximum physical fitness, no longer requiring glasses to see or a cane to walk.

DATA FILE

> Aldrich nonchalantly tells Pepper that five years spent with physical therapists are the reason he is now so changed.

> The desperation that Aldrich felt when Tony unkindly sent him up to a rooftop, to wait for a business meeting that never took place, nearly drove Aldrich to suicide.

Expertly tailored suit

Killian finds a new advantage of his exothermic power when seeking access to Rhodey's Iron Patriot suit. By touching the suit's armor and generating intense heat from his own body, Killian can effectively boil Rhodey until he gives in to torture and exits the suit—or, until the dangerous spike in temperature triggers the suit to open automatically.

On the oil tanker ship *Norco*, Stark's battle with Killian proves he is not quite a match for him. Although Tony, aided by his Iron Legion drones, can temporarily hinder Aldrich, Aldrich continues to overpower him by ripping units of armor from Tony's suits.

VENGEFUL MASTERMIND

Killian is driven by a mantra that Stark—a man who underestimated and ignored Killian—unknowingly taught him: the power of anonymity. Aldrich realizes that he can use this to hide behind a puppet villain, while he orchestrates events from behind the scenes. Vengeance also grips Aldrich, who enjoys taunting Tony over his inferior strength and inability to save Pepper.

Large dragon tattoos cover shoulders and chest

Exothermic energy glows through skin

Killian is furious to discover that his exothermic powers can actually be used tactically against him. Commanding a suit to encase the villain, Stark orders JARVIS to activate the suit's self-destruct mode—thus creating an almighty explosion, though it still fails to kill his foe.

Killian underestimates Pepper to his cost when he injects her with Extremis. Wearing a gauntlet from one of Tony's suits, Pepper uses a deadly combination of its repulsor and her new heat-generating powers to blast Killian into oblivion.

EXTREMIS

||||||||||||||||||||||||||||||||||||||||||||||||||||||||||||||

Defiant expression masks internal conflict

A scientific breakthrough gone horribly wrong, Extremis is a serum that chemically recodes living organisms' DNA, granting accelerated healing and repair, as well as enhanced strength and durability. Tested illegally on injured war veterans by Advanced Idea Mechanics (AIM), patients are able to channel heat at enormous temperatures; an unstable power that causes some test subjects to explode if their bodies reject the treatment. As the number of catastrophic explosions increase, AIM's CEO Aldrich Killian masterminds a theatrical plot to pass them off as terrorist bombings.

Extremis inventor Maya Hansen develops her research as part of Killian's think tank, AIM. Leading a team of 40 scientists, Hansen works in a gloomy, dungeon-like office, surrounded by laboratory equipment and a variety of plants—her original test subjects.

ERIC SAVIN

Arrogant and cocky, Eric Savin is an Extremis-powered henchman of Aldrich Killian. Savin regrows his foot after being caught in the explosion of an Extremis-addicted test subject. Nearly invulnerable, Savin is tasked with killing Tony Stark and proves a particularly tricky opponent to defeat.

Arms folded defensively

MAYA HANSEN

A visionary scientist, the highly gifted DNA coder Maya Hansen originally conceived Extremis as a method to heal life-threatening injuries and regrow lost limbs. In need of funding, Hansen joined AIM to continue her work. Now obsessed with finding a solution to stabilize Extremis, Hansen loses her moral compass in the quest for perfection, ignoring the dangers— something she eventually regrets as she begins to realize the monster she has helped to unleash.

> Slattery performs his Mandarin speeches from a throne in front of an ornate frieze depicting a pair of crossed guns.

> Aldrich entices Trevor Slattery to work for him with bribes of narcotics, plastic surgery, a mansion, and a "lovely speedboat."

Another of Killian's Extremis soldiers, Ellen Brandt, stalks Tony Stark in a vicious encounter. Walking through fire without flinching and rapidly healing her burned skin, Brandt demonstrates Extremis' capacity to block out pain.

The scale of the destruction becomes apparent to a suspicious Tony Stark as he surveys one of the recent explosion sites in Rose Hill, Tennessee. The force of the blast gouges a deep crater into the ground and kills six people.

PRESIDENT ELLIS
U.S. President Matthew Ellis is key to the Extremis plot. Aldrich Killian plans to kidnap him and execute him on live television, hoping to cause mass panic.

Long, scraggly beard

"THE MANDARIN"
Hired by Aldrich to pose as the public face of the so-called bombings, actor Trevor Slattery plays a menacing terrorist named the Mandarin in live broadcasts on hijacked television channels. Seduced by the glamor of a captive audience, lavish film set, and opulent pay package, the idiotic, bumbling Trevor is a far cry from his on-screen persona and does not realize the extent of Aldrich's villainy.

Bejeweled cuffs add to dramatic aura

Mandarin's costume of flowing green robes

Ornamental props

Gaudy rings adorn each finger

Fake gun (Slattery isn't trusted with a real one)

THOR

In an age long past, the people of Earth believed in a race of gods. These mighty beings would descend to the world to defend it from dark forces. Among them was one known as Thor, god of thunder. Like so many legends, these ones concealed a greater truth. These fearsome beings were real—aliens, not gods, for whom magic and technology were one and the same. Thor is their greatest warrior, and like those before him, he journeys to Earth to protect it from the forces of evil.

"I WOULD RATHER BE A GOOD MAN THAN A GREAT KING."

THOR ODINSON

THOR

Thor Odinson is the heir to the throne of Asgard and eventual ruler of its people. He is the son of King Odin and Queen Frigga, the younger brother of Hela, and older brother of Loki. Thor is a powerful warrior, whose conquests are legendary. His overconfidence, sense of entitlement, and rash decisions lead him down a path of self-discovery. Thor gains wisdom and learns to make personal sacrifices, both as an Avenger and a king.

With Odin due to go into a period of hibernation known as the Odinsleep, Thor is next in line for the throne. His coronation is a grand affair, assembling the entire kingdom. Thor feels worthy, but his recklessness will show he is not ready to be king.

GOD OF THUNDER

Like all Asgardians, Thor is blessed with supernatural strength and longevity. His strength, bravery, and mighty hammer gain him a reputation as the fiercest warrior in the Nine Realms. Thor boasts that he is the god of thunder, using Mjolnir to summon lightning at will, though it takes him time to understand the true nature of his power over storms.

Surface displays enchantments

Wooden handle with silver rings

MJOLNIR

Mjolnir was forged using the heart of a dying star. Thor uses it to summon lightning, smash adversaries, and as a powerful projectile weapon. Thor is able to fly by throwing the hammer and then holding onto its strap, and it will return to him when summoned. It can only be lifted by someone deemed worthy.

Symbol of Mjolnir

Long hair a symbol of warriors in Asgardian culture

Disks symbolize royal status

Bronze, steel, and leather cuirass

Hauberk of scale armor allows flexibility

Head forged from Uru metal

Cape of the Crown Prince of Asgard

Integrated knee guards

Bronze-plated leather boots

EXILE ON MIDGARD

In a childish rage, Thor breaks a peace treaty with the Frost Giants —one lasting more than a thousand years. Odin believes Thor has thoughtlessly endangered the lives of all Asgardians, so strips him of his power and banishes him to Midgard (Earth). Yet Odin will allow Thor to return—when he proves himself worthy. Thor's time on Midgard teaches him valuable lessons, and empathy with its people.

Pants belong to Dr. Jane Foster's ex, Donald Blake

MIDGARDIAN CLOTHES

Thor is still indignant when he lands in New Mexico. He demands to be brought back to Asgard but receives no answer. The first Midgardians that he encounters are a team of scientists led by Dr. Jane Foster.

As he banishes Thor, Odin throws Mjolnir to Midgard, too. Thor arrives at the temporary S.H.I.E.L.D. facility built around Mjolnir's crash site, and tries to lift the enchanted hammer. To his dismay, he realizes he is no longer worthy to lift it, and that he may remain exiled on Midgard forever.

Royal disks restored by Odin

Cap blocks Chitauri fire with his shield

BECOMING AN AVENGER

After his powers are restored, Thor considers Earth under his protection. When Loki arrives and then invades the planet with his Chitauri army, Thor feels a sense of duty and moral obligation to stop his adoptive brother. At first, his intervention puts him in conflict with the Avengers, as Thor wants to deal with Loki personally, but common goals make them natural allies once differences are resolved. Unlike the other members however, Thor's wider responsibilities in the galaxy require him to periodically leave Earth.

THOR:
TRIALS OF A GOD

After the events on Midgard (Earth), Thor realizes he is not yet ready to rule Asgard. First he must yet learn patience and humility. As a young warrior, he was prideful and focused only on achieving glory. He must now put the well-being of his people above his own desires. Thor faces a series of challenges that prove to both Odin and himself that he is ready to rule. Thor's adventures take him far, but finally lead him back to Asgard.

Mjolnir—poised for action

Strap for spinning hammer to gain momentum

Royal Asgardian cape

Thor often teams up with his brother, even though he knows he can't entirely trust him—Loki has tried to kill him several times, after all. Thor may achieve his goals, but whenever Loki is involved, there are always unintended consequences.

Thor's confidence in his own strength and his hammer leave him undaunted by powerful foes. On the planet Vanaheim, Thor faces a huge stone Kronan—the invading Marauders' strongest warrior. Thor dispatches him with a single blow.

Thor is used to being a leader in battle, but he must learn patience and deference as an Avenger. Thor and the Avengers work together to generate battle plans, while looking to Captain America for leadership.

GREATER CHALLENGES

Thor's adventures away from Asgard gain him the responsibility of protecting not only Earth, but also the entire universe. He stops the evil Dark Elf Malekith from plunging the whole universe into darkness, and helps the Avengers defeat the rogue android Ultron. But his jumbled visions of impending doom and the Infinity Stones concern him most.

Hair crudely shaved
by arena barber

Leather arm
bracers with
overlapping
plates

Hilt of one of a
pair of Sakaarian
gladiator swords

Super-strong
Asgardian muscles

Gladiator
war paint

Asgardian cape
now tattered
and dirty

Dust from
Sakaar's
Grand Arena

Thor's courage isn't limitless. For his introduction to the Grandmaster of Sakaar, Thor is strapped to a chair and forced through something akin to an automated theme park ride, causing him to scream in terror. Every new slave, gladiator, or plaything delivered to the Grandmaster goes through the same process.

FAMILY TROUBLE

Thor didn't know he had an older sister until Odin revealed the truth, just before his death. This leaves Thor unprepared when she suddenly appears, demanding he kneel in submission. Thor acknowledges that by birthright, Hela is the rightful heir to Odin's throne. Nonetheless, her evil nature makes her unworthy. Thor gets sidetracked into fighting as a gladiator on Sakaar, but when he finally does confront Hela, the resulting struggle destroys Asgard, and nearly destroys Thor and all of his people.

Thor has seen Black Widow calm Hulk many times by reaching out and sweet-talking him. When he attempts the same trick, he soon realizes, to his horror, that he doesn't have that magic touch.

Facing defeat at the hands of Hela, Thor suddenly realizes that his powers have always been inside him—they don't come from Mjolnir. With his self-confidence restored, Thor unleashes his full might against Hela's undead army.

LOKI

Prince Loki Odinson is the adopted son of King Odin and Queen Frigga of Asgard, and the younger brother of Thor. He was abandoned as a child by his biological father, King Laufey of the Frost Giants, because of his small (for his kind) size. Highly adept at magic, particularly illusion, Loki has earned the title "god of mischief." His selfish ambitions, jealousy, and rebellious nature create turmoil within his family, on Asgard, and on many worlds beyond.

Largest and heaviest of three gold helms

Blue Frost Giant skin transformed by Odin

Green is traditionally associated with trickery (and sometimes envy)

Solid gold cape clasp

Coronation regalia

Horns symbolize sorcery

LOKI'S HELM

PRINCE OF ASGARD

For years, Loki is unaware of his adoption or Frost Giant origins. He is raised as the son of Odin and Frigga, with all the rights and privileges of a prince of Asgard. Though Loki and his brother Thor squabble as children, an overt rivalry isn't apparent until after Thor's coronation. When Loki discovers his true origins, his feelings of resentment become uncontrollable.

Loki devises a scheme to prove his worth to Odin and usurp Thor's claim as heir to the throne. However, while Thor is banished to Midgard, Odin falls into the Odinsleep and Loki becomes next in line anyway. Loki didn't plan for this, but he certainly isn't complaining.

CASKET OF ANCIENT WINTERS
The Casket of Ancient Winters is a powerful relic that once belonged to Laufey, king of the Frost Giants. It has the power to send an entire world into an ice age. Long ago, when Odin defeated Laufey, he took the Casket to his vault on Asgard. Loki plans to use it to destroy Jotunheim and the Frost Giants who once abandoned him.

Pedestal of Fimbulvetr

DATA FILE

> Loki is skilled with a range of weapons, including his scepter and Odin's spear, Gungnir. However, his favorite weapons are daggers, which he wields with great dexterity.

> While in disguise in Germany, Loki transforms his scepter to look like an ostentatious walking cane.

> Whenever Loki touches Frost Giants or their relics, he temporarily reverts to his original form, with blue skin and red eyes.

Magic is Loki's preferred modus operandi. He uses it to change his appearance, cast doppelgangers, and communicate over vast distances. However, he will use force if he has to. His Frost Giant heritage makes him far stronger than any human.

INVADER OF EARTH

Following his brief but eventful reign, Loki abandons Asgard and ends up making a bargain with the Mad Titan Thanos. He agrees to recover the artifact known as the Tesseract for Thanos, in exchange for an army and a powerful scepter to conquer Earth. Deep down, Loki realizes he has made a bad deal. If he fails, Thanos will be angry, and even if his conquest is successful, at best he will still be Thanos' puppet.

Razor-sharp
blade

LOKI'S SCEPTER

Thanos gives Loki a scepter that allows him to control the minds of others. With it he can create brainwashed slaves and even an entire army.

Extendable
handle

Tough leather
shoulder protector

Containment vessel
for Mind Stone

Tarnished metal

Metal arm
guard with
embossed
design

Loki is highly intelligent and can concoct a plan to get out of any situation. When he is held prisoner on S.H.I.E.L.D.'s Helicarrier, he uses his mind-control powers to cause Hawkeye to attack the vessel. Then he triggers Banner's transformation into the Hulk, confident he can escape in the ensuing mayhem.

LOKI:
VILLAIN AND HERO

Loki wasn't always a villain. His misbehavior as a child resulted from an overwhelming desire to impress his father. Unfortunately, his efforts were invariably met by Odin's disapproval, leaving Loki frustrated and rebellious. As an adult, his lack of empathy means that even when his actions seem noble, his motives can be questioned; however, when Asgard is destroyed, he is largely responsible for saving his people.

Odin is merciful toward Loki after his failed attempt to conquer Earth, sending him to the dungeons of Asgard instead of executing him. Loki's cell is clean, spacious, and brightly lit.

GOD OF MISCHIEF

As a child, Loki was jealous of Thor's brute strength and boastfulness, and played cruel tricks on his brother. He eventually found another way of compensating for his inferiority complex. He learned magic from his mother, Frigga, and began using it to get an advantage—usually by playing tricks on others. Loki's mischievous nature coupled with his ever-growing ambition makes him highly unpredictable.

Neutral expression betrays no emotions

Familiar green color scheme

Scuffed bronze shoulder plate

Heavy armor hidden under quilted shirt

Hand reaches for concealed blade

Loki may lack Thor's strength, but he is no coward. He faces off with multiple Dark Elves on the desolation of Svartalfheim. As usual, however, his actions are not entirely selfless. He uses the opportunity to fake his own death in yet another bid for the throne.

DATA FILE

> When Frigga visits him in Asgard's dungeons, an enraged Loki lashes out at her, saying she is not really his mother. He doesn't actually mean it, and is torn apart when she is killed by the Dark Elves.

> Though Loki uses the situation for further advantage, his desire for vengeance on Kurse, his mother's killer, is genuine.

Ankle-length leather coat lined with green silk

ADVENTURES ON SAKAAR

When the Bifrost dumps Loki on the planet Sakaar, he ingratiates himself with the world's ruler and spends his days drinking, gambling, and indulging in all the palace has to offer. After Thor arrives and is immediately enslaved, Loki ignores his plight, only cooperating with his brother after his own exalted position is threatened by a revolt. His ability to manipulate people earns him a ride off the planet with a band of escaped gladiators, and he arrives at Asgard just in time to help Thor save their people from their evil sister, Hela.

Loki escapes from Sakaar unshaved (in contrast to Thor)

Seeking their father, Thor and Loki are transported by Doctor Strange to the coast of Norway. There, a dying Odin warns them of their sister's imminent arrival.

Loki arrives on Sakaar weeks before Thor. In that time he develops a cordial relationship with the planet's Grandmaster—one that he won't allow Thor to jeopardize.

Insignia grants access to Grandmaster's domains

Sakaarian double-bladed dagger

Tailored Sakaarian outfit made from arquindae leather

Cape is gift from Grandmaster

Old Asgardian leather boots

Ironically, Loki saves the Asgardians by destroying Asgard. On Thor's orders, he reunites the crown of the fire demon Surtur with the Eternal Flame in Odin's vault. The restored demon kills Hela but also annihilates Asgard, leaving its people homeless.

Energy feed for rifle

TEAMING UP

Self-preservation is Loki's most powerful motivator. Loki partners up with Thor to get off Sakaar, grabbing a weapon from a defeated palace guard. Rifles of this kind are normally used to keep Sakaar's Scrappers in line.

LADY SIF

Lady Sif is one of Asgard's greatest warriors, as well as one of Thor's closest friends. She and the so-called Warriors Three stand by Thor through his most difficult times, including his banishment to Earth. Sif is the most sensible of Thor's friends. She tries to talk him out of rash decisions but when his mind is made up, she loyally sides with Thor even at her own peril. Sif has feelings for Thor but she buries them deep. She would not do anything to jeopardize their friendship and she respects Thor's relationship with Jane Foster. Still, when Thor's mother, Frigga, wants insight into Thor's heart, it is Sif whom she asks, not Jane.

Sif has the courage to speak out when others hesitate. She warns Thor that provoking the Frost Giants is unwise, and she is proven painfully right. She still accompanies her friends to Jotunheim, though it is with the expectation that she may have to rescue them.

DATA FILE

> While Thor is on Midgard (Earth), Sif uses Heimdall's all-seeing cosmic vision to keep an eye on him.

> Celebrating after a great victory is an Asgardian tradition. Like her fighting skills, Sif's drinking skills make her a legend among her fellow warriors.

Sif and the Warriors Three visit the royal throne room expecting to petition Odin on Thor's behalf, but instead find Loki in full regalia, wielding Odin's spear. Loki's stance toward Thor is unmerciful.

RESPECTED WARRIOR

Before the elite Valkyrie were wiped out by Odin's daughter, Hela, female warriors were common in Asgard. Sif grew up in a different time, however. Some scoffed at the idea of a young maiden becoming one of the fiercest warriors Asgard has ever known. Sif spent most of her young life training with Thor, Hogun, Volstagg, and Fandral. In time, her martial prowess rises above the ranks of Odin's own Einherjar warriors and she is considered second in battle only to Thor.

BRINGING THOR HOME

Defying the command of Loki, Sif and the Warriors Three travel to Midgard to bring Thor home. Sif is elated to see her friend, who is unaware of the state of affairs at home.

Shirt of chain mail beneath cuirass

Multiple lames (overlapping plates) create articulated protection

Bracer wraps

Joined double pommel

Gold-plated fuller

Leather and chain-mail tasset skirt

Leather boots with silver highlights

Hands clutch pleadingly at Thor

Thor wears Midgardian clothes

BATTLE OF VANAHEIM

While Asgard's Bifrost bridge is out of action, alien Marauders take the opportunity to plunder the Nine Realms. As soon as the bridge is repaired, Sif and an Asgardian army travel to the world of Vanaheim to reclaim it. Her new armor gives her a greater range of motion in combat, and she slays many of the pillaging warriors. Sif's shield is not impervious to their harpoon rifles, however—it is ruined when Sif blocks a shot aimed at Thor.

SWORD AND SHIELD

Sif's enchanted sword has the ability to lengthen itself into a double-bladed spear. Odin has it reforged for her when it is damaged. Sif's sword and small shield lock together and are carried snugly on her forearm.

Menuki (grip ornaments)

Chappe (rain guard)

Arm raised for downward strokes

Chamfron (horse armor)

Decorative chain mail

Sif has fought in many battles alongside Thor and saved his life on more than one occasion. Despite Sif's feelings for Thor, her sense of duty to her friend and the realm never falter, even when she encounters Jane Foster on Asgard.

RIDING TO WAR

Sif rides into battle against the Marauders on her mighty steed, T'barr. The horse is kept in the royal stables near the castle on Vanaheim for her frequent visits.

Ornamental Asgardian knots

WARRIORS THREE

Thor's closest friends, apart from Sif, are the Warriors Three. Volstagg is Thor's most gregarious friend. His ax makes a good pairing with his larger-than-life personality. Fandral's sword suits his swashbuckling style—he is an adventurer at heart and fancies himself a ladies' man. Hogun is the most introverted, but he wields a brutish bludgeon. It transforms from an unthreatening scepter into a spiked mace— all with just a simple hand twist.

VOLSTAGG

When Loki sends the Destroyer to kill his brother on Midgard, Thor's loyal friends come to his aid. Their weapons are no match for the enchanted automaton, however.

HOGUN'S MACE

Mace in flail mode

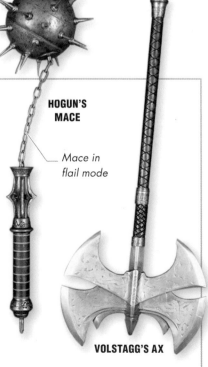

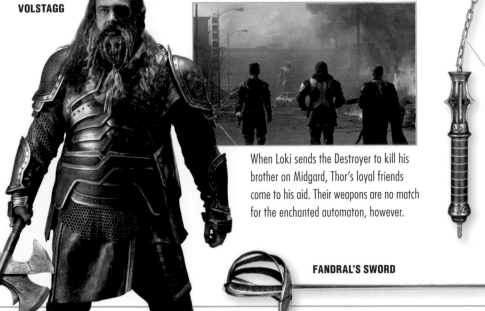

FANDRAL'S SWORD

VOLSTAGG'S AX

ODIN

Odin is the king of Asgard. He is the son of Bor and grandson of Buri, as well as the father of Hela, Thor, and Loki. Odin claims the titles of allfather and god of wisdom, though he concedes to his sons that they are merely powerful mortals and not divine. Odin is the greatest warrior in the kingdom (until Thor takes on that mantle) and has battled enemies across the Nine Realms, including on Earth. Odin can be stern but he is also just and merciful. He is quick to make peace treaties and his punishments tend to have clauses for restoration.

Odin's judgments seem harsh to Thor when he is on the receiving end, but they always have a purpose. Odin uses tough love to teach Thor valuable life lessons.

Eye lost in battle with Frost Giants

Ceremonial royal cape

Energy blasts fired from center

GUNGNIR

Odin's spear is the symbol of Asgardian kingship and was borne by his father Bor before him. Made of Uru metal, it wields great power over the realm of Asgard, including control of the Bifrost bridge and the guardian automaton known as the Destroyer.

Odin's war regalia

SLEIPNIR, ODIN'S WARHORSE

KING OF ASGARD

Odin was not always a benevolent king. In his early centuries he was a conqueror. Once he established the Nine Realms he sought peace and prosperity, but the ambition of his daughter and war general, Hela, was unquenchable. He banished Hela after she attempted a coup. Centuries later, he grooms his eldest son, Thor, to take his place as ruler.

Sleipnir has eight legs

Shimmering gold weave crafted by Asgard's finest artisans

DEFENDER OF THE REALMS

As king of Asgard it is Odin's duty to ensure the protection of the Nine Realms. The security of these worlds must be ensured above any single person. Sometimes Thor is frustrated by what he sees as Odin's inaction, because Thor doesn't see the bigger picture. In the later years of Odin's reign, Odin is more concerned about preserving peace than seeking vengeance and retribution, and he passes this outlook on to Thor.

DATA FILE

> Odin's two pet ravens, Hugin and Munin, bring him news from throughout the Nine Realms. They remain by his side during Odinsleep (Odin's periodic hibernations).

> When Thor is banished or Loki rebels, Odin sends the ravens to watch over his boys.

Frigga has a habit of petitioning Odin on behalf of both her children. His stubbornness can infuriate her, but ultimately she believes Odin will always make the right decision.

After her death, Frigga is given an Asgardian funeral. She is placed in ceremonial armor on a longboat, which is then set ablaze.

FRIGGA

Queen Frigga is Odin's wife and the mother of Thor and Loki. Her family is more important to her than anything else. Frigga is a skilled sorceress and uses magic to visit Loki even when Odin sentences him to prison. Selfless to the end, she is killed by the Dark Elf Algrim while protecting Jane Foster.

Curls piled into regal updo

Yellow diamond from Alfheim

Lustrous gemstones from Vanaheim

Coronation gown

ASGARD

IIIIIIIIIIIIIIIIIIIIIIIIIIIIIIIIIIIIIIIIIIIIIIIIIIIIIIIIIIIIIIIIIIIIII

Asgard is the homeworld of Thor and the Asgardian people.
It is also the capital of the Nine Realms connected by Yggdrasil
(the cosmic World Tree). Asgard is an unusual planetary body,
sprawling outward from a central island on a double-sided plane.
Asgard has gravity, a breathable atmosphere, and cyclical days
and nights. The beautiful topside is inhabited by King Odin and
his people—a heavenly domain that is the envy of the galaxy.
The underside, however, is an icy, mountainous country
that is much less welcoming.

Auto-tracking turret

CITY DEFENSES

Asgard's defenses include large
cannons mounted on turrets
throughout the city, royal skiffs, and a
palace shield that can be activated by
Heimdall from his Bifrost observatory.

Royal City

Stone
watchtower

Water cascades
over the edge
into space

ROYAL CAPITAL

The City of Asgard is the sole municipality of
Asgard. The splendorous metropolis has stood
for thousands of years. The royal domain includes
the palace at the city center, the royal aviary and
stables, armory, Einherjar barracks with its monument
to the Valkyrie, the dungeons, and the Bifrost bridge.
The city is a place where art and learning are
celebrated as are the deeds of valiant warriors.
Advanced technology and ageless architectural
grandeur blend as one.

DATA FILE

> The weather is always pleasant in Asgard.
The city exists in perpetual springtime, where
blossom and harvest both coincide.

> The Asgardians use hovercraft known as
skiffs for rapid travel across Asgard, and also
as military gunships.

Royal Palace

Rainbow Bridge
(Bifrost)

The City of Asgard is
nestled in a fertile valley
facing the sea. Vineyards
grow along the foothills
and fishermen cast nets
close to shore.

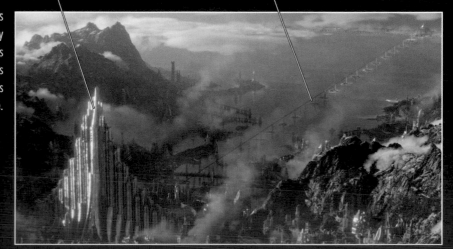

Asgard's mountainous countryside is pristine. Snowy peaks descend into
valleys carved by waterfalls. Lush forests are home to Habrok hawks
and four species of deer: Dainn, Duneyrr, Durapror, and Dvalinn.

Face emits blasts
of white-hot energy

**EINHERJAR
SHIELD**

Deflects dark-
energy particles
and other munitions

Armor is
~~pervious to~~
almost all
known
weapons

Bluish-gray
cape

THE PALACE

The Royal Palace of Valaskjalf, where Odin and his
family dwell, is an immense structure, appearing like golden
organ pipes towering above the city. Odin keeps valuable
treasures in his vault—treasures he fears might cause untold
destruction in the wrong hands. These include the Casket of
Ancient Winters, the Eternal Flame, the Warlock's Eye, and
the Infinity Gauntlet (though the latter is really a fake).

THE DESTROYER

Odin's vault is protected by a powerful, almost
indestructible automaton known simply as the
Destroyer. It obeys whoever holds Odin's spear,
Gungnir. Loki sends it against his brother during
Thor's banishment to Earth, but an act of
self-sacrifice allows Thor to defeat it.

THE EINHERJAR

Asgard's elite army is known as the Einherjar.
In times of peace, they serve as the palace guard.
Sadly, Hela—Odin's firstborn—wipes them all
out when she returns to claim the throne.

Remnant stone of
the horse Skinfaxi

THRONE OF ASGARD

One of a pair of
stylized raven
guardians

Stone of
Hrimfaxi

Limbs can
rotate and
change shape

Solid gold steps
leading to dais

Odin's throne is known
as the Hlidskjalf. He sits
flanked by his two ravens,
with Gungnir—his mighty
spear and the symbol of
kingship—by his side.

A prophecy foretells that Asgard will end in Ragnarok.
This will occur when the fire demon Surtur is resurrected
by the Eternal Flame and then destroys Asgard. What
the prophecy does not say, is that Thor is the one who
sets these dreadful events in motion.

HEIMDALL

Heimdall is the sentinel of Asgard and the guardian of the Bifrost—Asgard's gateway to the Nine Realms and beyond. His supernatural eyesight allows him to see to the far reaches of the cosmos, a gift he uses to keep tabs on both friends and enemies on other planets. Heimdall is an honorable hero who is loyal to both the family of Odin and the people of Asgard. He helps Thor find an escape route when he gets trapped on Sakaar and he is responsible for his people's survival and exodus from Asgard during Hela's short, bloody reign.

Large helm meant to intimidate

Bull-like horns

Bronze pommel

HEIMDALL'S HELMS

Heimdall has more than one helm. Each is designed to resemble a great, immovable bull (or tarfr). It is said that he who wears such a helm cannot be displaced.

Heavy cuirass protects from Bifrost energy

Heimdall has a strong bond with members of the royal family. He meets Thor in a cozy tavern in the city. The walls are lined with shields and a roaring fire is stoked by the bartender.

Hofund, Heimdall's enchanted sword

GATEKEEPER

The Bifrost is the only way to leave Asgard (for all but Loki), as Odin keeps no starships. Thus Heimdall's administration of the Bifrost is essential for travel. It allows Asgard's warriors to police the Nine Realms and for trade to exist between them. Heimdall keeps watch from his Observatory for approaching ships, and also potential problems developing on other worlds that could later threaten Asgard.

Soft ox leather tasset

Bronze-framed leather tabard

THE BIFROST

Heimdall's Observatory, or Himinbjorg, is situated at the end of the Rainbow Bridge on the precipice of Asgard. It is from here that the Bifrost is projected. The Bifrost itself is a bridge of energy that allows rapid travel to any of the Nine Realms and Asgardian protectorates located along Yggdrasil (the World Tree). Heimdall is its official guardian, but in times of turmoil others may fill in for him.

Heimdall always does what he thinks is right, even if it means disobeying orders. This has put him at odds with Asgard's rulers, including Odin, Loki, and Hela.

Sword is 5 ft 4 in (1.6 m) long

The Rainbow Bridge is more than a road from the city to Heimdall's Observatory. It is a conduit of energy that powers the Bifrost. When Thor destroys it to stop Loki, the Bifrost is rendered temporarily unusable.

FUGITIVE

When Loki masquerades as Odin, he has Heimdall put on trial as a traitor. Loki knows Heimdall can see everything—including through his own deception—so needs him out of the way. Heimdall escapes to Asgard's mountains, which has the added benefit of allowing him to avoid Hela when the exiled princess arrives on Asgard and slaughters the Bifrost's new custodians. Heimdall finds himself without his armor and wears simple garb to blend in. He uses his vantage to hold out for Thor's return and fight for Asgard from the shadows.

When Hela takes over Asgard, Heimdall is the only one left to protect the people. He gathers them in an ancient stronghold up in the mountains. The rock fortress served the people in troll invasions long ago and Heimdall keeps the people here until Hela discovers their refuge.

Golden eyes see across Nine Realms

Dragon leather bracers

Heimdall bravely protects the people from Hela's army of undead soldiers. His sword is not just for show and opening the Bifrost—Heimdall is a near-matchless swordsman and warrior.

Old blanket from Vanaheim

Blade never needs sharpening

Pocket contains fire-starter tools

Heimdall may see across the universe, but some things can still be obscured from him. The Dark Elves' cloaking devices keep their ship invisible to Heimdall until it is almost on top of him.

Ox-leather pants

Sentinel's leather boots

OPENING THE BIFROST

Only two weapons may open and close the Bifrost: Heimdall's sword, Hofund, and Odin's spear, Gungnir. If the Bifrost is left open too long, its vast power can destroy an entire world. Hofund itself seems to retain some of the powers of the Bifrost after Asgard is obliterated.

Bifrost lock

DATA FILE

> Heimdall warns of approaching danger by blowing the Gjallerhorn. This ancient instrument can be heard across Asgard.

> Heimdall's cosmic vision gives him a more sweeping perspective of events than most beings.

THOR'S ALLIES

Astrophysicist Dr. Jane Foster, her colleague Dr. Erik Selvig, and intern Darcy Lewis are out in the desert near Puente Antiguo, New Mexico, investigating a recurring meteorological phenomenon when they first meet Thor. Foster's scientific curiosity leads her into supernatural danger, first from the Asgardian Destroyer, and later Dark Elves and their cosmic doomsday device. A fiery romance with Thor grows but eventually fizzles out, the cosmic distances proving too great.

Outfit borrowed from Frigga

Asgardian sapphire dress

Silver-plated etched cuirass

Cushioned gauntlet

Thor teaches Jane about the world tree Yggdrasil and the Nine Realms linked by it. The romance between them grows as Thor tells her tales of the wonders beyond Earth.

Notebook of observations about Bifrost phenomenon

DR. JANE FOSTER

Foster graduated from Culver University, Virginia, where her father and Dr. Selvig worked together. Inquisitive and impulsive by nature, Jane is not easily swayed by others, and is unafraid to take risks that could lead her into peril, or to fall foul of the authorities. Following her adventures with Thor, Foster's newfound knowledge leads her to becomes the world's leading astrophysicist, and a candidate for the Nobel Prize.

Practical jacket layered over plaid shirt for warmth during fieldwork

SCIENCE IN THE FIELD

Foster finds scientific experiments in the field much more exciting than theoretical research in a lab. Foster's desire to work outside the office allows her to meet Thor, but it also leads her into great danger.

When Jane is infected by the Aether—the Dark Elves' doomsday weapon—Thor brings her to Asgard for treatment. Standing on a palace balcony over the water, he explains the Convergence of the Nine Realms, which occurs every 5,000 years.

Dr. Selvig is initially skeptical of Darcy Lewis' scientific abilities, but he later works closely with her after she is the first to note an anomaly on a photograph that proves Thor's presence on Earth.

DR. ERIK SELVIG

Selvig is a former professor of theoretical astrophysics at Culver University, and a mentor to Jane Foster. After helping Thor during his banishment, Erik goes on to work for S.H.I.E.L.D., where he gets caught up in Loki's invasion of Earth. For a while, Selvig is left disturbed by the trauma of being subjected to Loki's prolonged mind control. It takes him considerable time and a stint at a psychiatric institution to return to his old self, but his brilliance is demonstrated once again when his gravimetric spike technology helps save Earth from the Dark Elves.

Regular (if slightly disheveled) clothes replace odd hospital garb

In the asylum, Selvig's calculations for the Convergence are a jumble of fringe theories, including the Nexus of All Reality, the 616 Universe, Simpson's Theory of Relativity, the "Fault" in the fabric of the universe, and the "Crossroads" to other worlds.

After Erik embarks on a series of naked public escapades, it is a relief for Darcy and her intern, Ian, to retrieve him from the asylum. As they leave, they see a flock of disappearing birds—indicating the Convergence is about to take place.

Woolly hat for chilly London weather

DARCY LEWIS

Lewis is the unpaid intern (for which she receives six college credits) and assistant of Dr. Foster and Dr. Selvig. The loyal political science student helps them when Thor first arrives on Earth, and then later when the Dark Elves threaten to destroy the universe. She is bright and ambitious, and even takes on an intern of her own, Ian Boothby.

Darcy is surprisingly unfazed by Thor and has no misgivings about interrupting him and Jane during intimate moments.

Bag full of gravimetric spike parts to counter effect of Convergence

DATA FILE

> Working on Project PEGASUS, Dr. Selvig inadvertently helps destabilize the Tesseract, opening a portal for Loki to arrive on Earth.

> Jane and her colleagues first encounter Thor when they accidentally run him over with their truck/mobile laboratory.

THE NINE REALMS

The Nine Realms are an association of nine planetary bodies under the jurisdiction of Asgard. The worlds and their respective inhabitants include Alfheim (Light Elves), Asgard (Asgardians), Jotunheim (Frost Giants), Midgard (Humans), Muspelheim (Fire Demons), Nidavellir (Dwarves), Niflheim (Hela), Svartalfheim (Dark Elves), and Vanaheim (Vanir). Odin's daughter, Hela, helped him conquer them all, but she rebelled when Odin resolved to halt his conquest at just the Nine Realms.

Fiery realm of
Muspelheim

Much of Asgard's wealth was taken from realms conquered by Odin—a history that is now kept concealed.

THE CONVERGENCE

An event known as the Convergence occurs across the Nine Realms every 5,000 years. It allows momentary travel between the Nine Reams via portals, without use of the Bifrost. The Convergence was the event that first alerted ancient humans to the existence of other realms, and the alien life found there.

FROST GIANTS

Jotuns, or Frost Giants, are powerful, long-lived beings. They are able to manipulate ice at will, especially to form weapons and alter the landscape.

Pattern of ridges is unique
to each Frost Giant

KING LAUFEY

Skin so cold it
causes instant
frostbite if touched

Armor made
from jade stone

The Asgardian *Book of Yggdrasil* foretells the Convergence. It describes it as the time when the branches of the cosmic world tree Yggdrasil become intertwined.

Lush forests
of Vanaheim

JOTUNHEIM

The Frost Giants are ancient enemies of Asgard. They live on the frozen world of Jotunheim, in long-ruined strongholds. Jotunheim persists in an endless winter night, a chilling wasteland home to fearsome ice wargs and great frost beasts. The inhabitants are unwelcoming to Asgardians and humans, who are likely to be eaten once discovered.

YGGDRASIL

The Nine Realms are connected by an invisible "World Tree" known as Yggdrasil. Its limbs form cosmic pathways that connect the worlds. Yggdrasil is an important symbol in Asgardian culture, representing the galaxy and the interconnectedness of its planets and people.

Icy mountains of Jotunheim

DATA FILE

> Thor is briefly held captive on Muspelheim. His imprisonment is a ruse to discover the fire demon Surtur's weaknesses.

> Loki kills his Jotun father, King Laufey, to save Odin, the adoptive father who loved and raised him.

Edge of cosmic portal

Ancient Anorag corsair helmet

Methane breathing apparatus

Armor taken from a Baluurian warrior

Crude steel ax

MIDGARD

Asgardians and beings from the other realms have been visiting Midgard (also known as Earth) for thousands of years. The ancient Norse were aware of these visitors and some believed the aliens were gods. Other visitors inspired legends of giants, trolls, and elves. The Frost Giants tried to wipe out humanity and colonize Midgard in 965 BCE, but Odin came to the rescue and defeated them in Tønsberg, Norway.

Looted smuggler's jacket

MARAUDERS

The Marauders are the scourge of the Nine Realms. They are a collective of loosely affiliated alien pirates, composed of many different races, including R'malk'Is, Yrds, Kronans, Sakaarans, and Easiks. They ruthlessly raid settlements in large groups, often working across multiple star systems until settling on a profitable world to set up as a comfortable base of operations.

Scavenged pilot's glove

DARK ELVES

The Dark Elves are one of the oldest known races, born in darkness before the dawn of the present universe. The elves were once a peaceful race who lived on a world of serene beauty. When the present universe arose—one that thrives on light and a new set of atomic elements—its existence threatened their own. Their evil leader, Malekith, waits patiently for an event called the Convergence, when once every 5,000 years all Nine Realms blend one into another. Then he will unleash an awesome destructive force known as the Aether, which will convert reality to an endless night of dark matter and dark energy.

Face burned by Thor's lightning

Life-support suit

Symbol is reminder of ancient battle wound

Heavy, corroded gauntlet

After slumbering for millennia, Malekith awakens aboard his Ark ship floating in deep space. He and his minions are alerted when the Aether is discovered by Dr. Jane Foster, just in time for the Convergence.

MALEKITH

Malekith is spiteful and malevolent. He could use the infinitely powerful Aether to create an isolated safe haven for the Dark Elves to live, but instead he seeks to plunge the entire cosmos back into darkness and destroy all other life. He is so fanatical and self-serving in his quest, that he is willing to sacrifice all of his people to have revenge upon the very light of the universe.

Malekith arrives at the Old Royal Naval College in the Greenwich borough of London. The scenic location on the River Thames is the focal point of the Convergence of the Nine Realms, linking them all through overlapping portals.

DATA FILE

> The Aether is at least partially sentient; when it believes its host is threatened, it will lash out violently to protect itself.

> The Aether grants Malekith powerful telekinetic abilities. It also makes him impervious to most weapons.

ASGARDIAN WARNINGS

The illuminated *Book of Yggdrasil* in Odin's library tells the story of the Dark Elves. The pages magically animate to depict the elves fighting the light by building a weapon called the Aether, supposedly formed from darkness itself.

The Dark Elves' homeworld is called Svartalfheim. Located in a quadrant rich with dark matter, the planet's only light comes from a dying star being consumed by a black hole. Svartalfheim was laid waste by a war with King Bor and the Asgardians. After his victory, Bor concealed the Aether beneath the planet's surface, where it is later found by Jane Foster.

Rifle barrel

Particle inversion chamber

Supporting hand position

Firing hand position

Mask lenses protect light-sensitive eyes

DARK ELF SOLDIERS

The state of the present universe is toxic to Dark Elves. The light, air, and the very matter essential to most life is poisonous to them. Dark Elves wear survival suits and masks to survive in what they refer to as the "wretched new universe." Their masks resemble their appearance as it once was, before they were corroded by toxins. Malekith's soldiers are the last of their kind—though most are killed when he is defeated, a few specimens may remain, scattered elsewhere by Dr. Selvig's gravimetric spikes.

PARTICLE RIFLE

Dark Elf technology is powered by dark energy and black holes. Their particle rifles are ancient weapons that fire lethal blasts of dark matter particles. On impact, these particles tear apart living tissue at a molecular level.

Dark-energy core

BLACK HOLE GRENADE

Living mask fused to face

Dark Elf sword

Main bridge

"KURSE"

Malekith sends his lieutenant, Algrim, to infiltrate Asgard on a mission to deactivate the palace's shield generator. Once inside, he uses a Kurse Stone to transform into a monstrous beast consumed by darkness.

Boot protects foot from caustic matter

MALEKITH'S ARK

The battleships of the Dark Elves are known as Arks. Malekith's is the only one that survived the previous war with Asgard. Arks are equipped with cloaking devices and they can carry Harrow fighters. They are capable of holding hundreds of soldiers and maintaining them in hibernation for millennia.

The Aether is actually the Reality Stone—one of the six Infinity Stones, though unlike the others, it is often in liquid form. At the precise moment of the Convergence, Malekith unleashes it. His goal is at hand—to revert the universe to the darkness from which he was born.

SAKAAR

Sakaar is literally the dump of the galaxy. Fissures in space and time (commonly called wormholes) deposit not only garbage here but also beings of all kinds, including some with extraordinary abilities. The planet is governed by an affable tyrant known as the Grandmaster. His world is far from other habitable planets and the surrounding anomalies make it difficult to leave orbit. The so-called Devil's Anus is the largest wormhole in the sky and the fastest way to Asgard. However, as the collapsing neutron star inside a wormhole tends to spit out anyone foolish enough to enter—usually in small pieces— those unlucky enough to find themselves on Sakaar seldom leave.

On his way to Asgard, Thor is knocked out of the Bifrost beam and falls to Sakaar's junk-covered surface. He finds himself in a bizarre cityscape cobbled together from portions of old space freighters, shipping containers, and derelict space stations.

Feeding tube

SCRAPPERS

Scrappers are Sakaar's local scavengers, descendants of travelers who arrived on Sakaar via the wormholes. Their clothing is a melding of cultural garb from across the galaxy, with masks, colors, and patterns representing their clans and tribes. Scrappers are armed with magno-rifles, clubs, and nets. Any living thing they catch is a potential meal, slave, or gladiator.

Jury-rigged magno-rifle

JUNK PLANET

As a nexus of cosmic conduits, Sakaar's sky is a sieve of the galaxy's veritable garbage chutes and sewage pipes. The planet's surface is composed of wreckage from the wars between Xandar and the Kree Empire, rotting Celestial body parts, and ships that wander just a little too close. All of Sakaar's resources—even sustenance—come from the extraterrestrial refuse deposited by the wormholes. Above it all looms the Grandmaster's palace, perching him over the squalor, yet ever-present in the daily lives of his people.

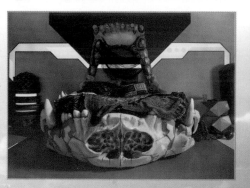

The Grandmaster has given his favorite champion—the Hulk—a lavish suite in his tower with a view of the Kirby Residential Spires. Hulk gets whatever he wants for his room, including a hot tub, a Hulk-sized minibar, exercise equipment, and a bed made from the overturned skull of one of his conquests, a thundering mustelagon.

Grandmaster's palace

Tower of Champions

Wormhole

Grand Arena

Kirby Residential Spires

Sakaarian Guard barracks

MELTING STICK

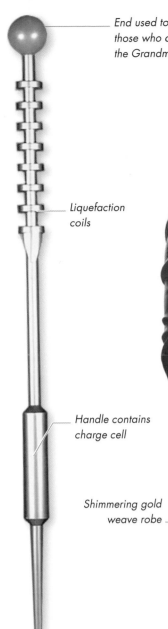

End used to "pardon" those who displease the Grandmaster

Liquefaction coils

Handle contains charge cell

Shimmering gold weave robe

Hairstyle of the day

Blue facial markings supposedly symbolize wisdom

Ring set with mysterious gem

Sleeve for concealing surprises

Scavenged from luxury cruise ship

Blue toenail polish matches fingernails

THE GRANDMASTER

The Grandmaster was the first to arrive on Sakaar and is credited as its creator. As ruler, he must maintain a delicate balance: his people are stranded for eternity in a giant garbage dump and could be crushed at any time by debris falling from the sky. To keep his subjects at ease, and prevent mass hysteria from breaking out, the Grandmaster must keep them distracted and jubilant. He makes this difficult task look easy thanks to his Contest of Champions and many festivals. How he intends to pacify the populace once they do revolt remains to be seen.

The Grandmaster spends a lot of time having fun in his various party rooms. When Thor arrives, he discovers that Loki has already been partying here for weeks. Time passes differently on Sakaar—a phenomenon caused by the surrounding wormholes. The Grandmaster has been here so long that on any other world, he would be millions of years old.

LORD OF HEDONISM

As one of the oldest beings in the universe, the Grandmaster has had a lot of leisure time, and hasn't spent it reputably.

TOPAZ

The Grandmaster's most trusted lieutenant and right-hand woman is Topaz, the head of the Sakaarian Guard. She's smart, doesn't take insults from anyone, always speaks her mind, and has a dark sense of humor. She enjoys her special status and resents Scrapper #142's inroads with the Grandmaster.

Topaz is the best pilot in the Sakaarian Guard. She finds shooting down non-compliant Scrapper ships highly therapeutic.

Sakaarian facial markings

Gauntlet projects holographic view screen

All the best spirits found or produced on Sakaar go to the Grandmaster. One of the biggest perks in finding favor with him is getting access to the many minibars around the palace.

CONTEST OF CHAMPIONS

The Contest of Champions is the brainchild of Sakaar's tyrannical ruler, the Grandmaster. It is a brutal contest where gladiators fight to the death as entertainment. Scrapper #142 brought him the current reigning champion, "The Incredible Hulk," and is paid 10 million units for delivering Thor. The Grandmaster likes to gamble on his fights, and will do anything to keep from losing. He promises that any contender who defeats his champion will gain their freedom, but when the "Lord of Thunder" is about to win, the Grandmaster sabotages him. Thor is forced to find another way to freedom, and makes a few gladiator friends in the process.

The Grandmaster's palace is adorned with giant sculptures showing the faces of his greatest champions. The newest addition is the Hulk, who is still under construction.

"LORD OF THUNDER"

Over the course of two days, Thor loses both his father and Mjolnir, is captured on Sakaar, and then watches the Grandmaster melt someone into a steaming blue puddle in front of him. The Grandmaster disrespects Thor, calling him "Sparkles" and "Lord of Thunder," before making him a gladiator slave.

Toughened cuirass

Segmented blades can change shape

Helmet's wings have sharpened edges

Ordinary belt buckle replaces lost magic one

Red war paint spells "Lord of Thunder" in Sakaarian symbols

Boots provide good grip in dust of arena floor

Ribbed handles for extra grip

THOR'S ARENA SWORDS

THOR'S ARENA HELMET

Blades are compacted when inside scabbards

GLADIATOR GLAMOUR
Fully extended, the swords that Thor chooses are 3 ft (0.9 m) long. They are a blend of utility and technology, with shape-shifting blades based on the wings of a fighting insect. Fittingly, Thor's helmet is an Asgardian-inspired design. It can be used as a weapon itself—the bladed "wings" can be deadly if positioned properly for a headbutt.

Blunt edges to limit lethal injuries

Thor waits anxiously in the arena as 400,000 spectators look on. He is relieved to find that the Grandmaster's champion is his friend Hulk, but is confused when Hulk attacks him.

DATA FILE

> While Thor may be the god of thunder, he is not impervious to electricity and can be knocked out by a powerful shock from the obedience disk implanted into his neck.

> Bruce Banner has been dormant inside the Hulk for two years. He is in danger of losing himself and becoming Hulk permanently.

> Hulk's arena weapons are huge. His hammer weighs approximately 295 lbs (134 kg)—the equivalent of two adult men.

Doug's crest

SECOND-HAND GEAR

Thor feels lost without his hammer, and choosing between unfamiliar armaments proves difficult. The weapons themselves are unconventional, too; they are designed to entertain the crowds and maim opponents, but not kill too hurriedly. He settles on gear once owned by an ill-fated gladiator named Doug.

Ultra-dense handle acts as counterweight

THOR'S MACE

Protects lower body

THOR'S SHIELD

Body made of perishable rock

KORG

Beings come from far and wide to participate (unwillingly) in the Contest of Champions. Each has an obedience disk implanted in their neck, which will shock them if they stop complying. Korg is the friendly Kronan leader of these gladiators. His people are made of stone and hail from the planet Ria, a protectorate of Asgard. Korg led a failed rebellion and was sentenced to fight in the arena as punishment.

Rocks continually fall away from body and are replaced by newly formed ones (like dead skin)

Like all gladiators on Sakaar, Thor is put in a grim holding cell before pre-match processing. As Thor discovers, the cell is a sealed ring of space-time from which escape is impossible.

BATTLING HULK

Thor has a history of dispatching massive foes with comparative ease, so he stands a decent chance against Hulk. The crowd is used to Hulk smashing his foes rapidly, and they are confused when the fight starts to turn against him. Thor is on the verge of winning when the Grandmaster activates the obedience disk in Thor's neck, incapacitating him.

HELA

||||||||||||||||||||||||||||

Hela is the elder sister Thor and Loki never knew they had… or ever wanted. A skilled general and bloodthirsty warrior, she was Odin's most powerful weapon in the conquest of the Nine Realms. After he achieved his goals, a remorseful Odin ushered in a time of peace. Hela, who styles herself as the goddess of death, refused to yield, so Odin banished her. Thor and Loki discover to their cost that Hela is virtually invincible—she draws her immense power from Asgard itself, and only Ragnarok, the prophesied destruction of Asgard, can stop her.

Headdress forms at will

Antlers change shape depending on intention

Hela's outfit repairs itself as her power is restored

Blades pierce but cannot kill Hela

Hands open to summon weaponry

Mantle of Darkness

Necro-energy courses through Hela's clothing

Following Odin's death, Hela returns to claim her throne and introduces herself to her brothers. Her hair is bedraggled and clothing torn from her inhospitable exile. Yet Hela's power stuns Thor when she crushes Mjolnir, his mighty hammer, like a piece of glass.

ODIN'S FIRST-BORN

Hela truly is Odin's first child, that is no lie. Unlike Loki, she has no need for deceit in her pursuit of the throne; she is entitled to it by birthright. If Odin had not banished her, she would almost certainly have taken the throne by force long ago. To Hela, Asgard is merely a place: the source of her power and a realm to be reclaimed. Asgard's people are of no consequence to her.

Hela is incensed that Asgardians have not been taught their true blood-soaked history, and know nothing of her conquests. Still, she does them the courtesy of introducing herself and inviting them to serve her. When the Einherjar (the army of Asgard) stand firm, she decimates them with ease.

Hair-splitting blade edge

Backward-facing hooks make dislodging blades difficult

Glowing with necro-energy

NECROSWORD

Chalice of Muspelheim

ETERNAL FLAME

The Eternal Flame is a mystical, inextinguishable flame that holds the power of the Fire Demon Surtur. Due to its prophesied role in Asgard's destruction, it is kept under guard in Odin's vault.

Pillar of Privaldi

RIDE OF THE VALKYRIE

After Hela was first banished to the region known as Hel, she opened a portal and tried to fight her way back into the palace on Asgard. Odin sent the Valkyrie, his greatest warriors, to stop her. Amidst the cold gloom and rocky landscape they all fell to Hela's flurry of necroswords—all except one warrior who managed to escape. Odin resealed the rift, abandoning Hela until his own death, when his power would no longer be able to contain her.

DATA FILE

> Hela's old army is buried in a massive crypt beneath Odin's vault. Hela reanimates her long-dead troops with the Eternal Flame.

> Hela's zombie soldiers are known as Dead Guards or Butchers. They helped her conquer the Nine Realms millennia ago.

WEAPON MANIFESTATION

Hela has a gory power: she can summon an infinite supply of deadly weapons. These include axes and spikes, but she prefers hurling blades of varying lengths.

Unstoppable blade tip

NECROBLADES

Coarse hair smells like death

FENRIS

Hela's 35 ft (11 m) long steed and furry companion is Fenris, a ferocious war wolf. Like her undead army, Hela restores him to life with the Eternal Flame. Unlike Hela's soldiers, however, Fenris regains his natural vitality. Fenris' skin is bulletproof and his teeth are like knives; even able to puncture Hulk's leg.

Hela approaches Thor and Loki on the Bifrost, where they make their final stand. Her near-limitless power makes her overconfident— she never imagines that the heroes would intentionally bring about Ragnarok to destroy her.

VALKYRIE

Valkyrie, or "Scrapper #142" as she is known on Sakaar, is a bounty hunter who captures and sells prospective gladiators to the planet's Grandmaster. She is a former Valkyrie; an all-female regiment of Asgardian warriors sworn to protect the throne. When Odin's fearsome daughter, Hela, grew beyond his control, Hela started a coup and slaughtered everyone in the palace. Odin banished Hela, but she tried—unsuccessfully—to return, killing Valkyrie's entire unit in the process. Distraught at the loss of her comrades, Valkyrie left Asgard and settled on Sakaar as Scrapper #142.

Scrapper #142 spends a lot of time at the bar by the gladiator armory, where party-bot servers dispense cheap drinks made from unthinkable fermented ingredients. Drinking to bury her past, she is unsympathetic to Thor's plight or the fates of the other gladiators.

Valkyrie doesn't like Thor getting familiar. It forces her to confront unpleasant memories. Despite his pleas, she refuses to help. She is fed up with people dying in Odin's family squabbles.

Tough soles for climbing over junk piles

Gauntlets remotely control Warsong's guns

Silver-gilded leather belt

Leather tasset

DRAGONFANG

The swords of the Valkyrie are legendary and unique to each warrior. The design and shape of Valkyrie's sword, Dragonfang, harkens back to earlier Asgardian weapons used during Odin's violent conquest of the Nine Realms.

Dragonhide strap

Black sapph can be plac in pommel

Carved dragon's tooth hilt

Black ceramic locket

Sakaarian Scrapper face paint markings

Tattered Valkyrie cape

Sapphiric steel blade

SCABBARD

BLADE

BOUNTY HUNTER

When Valkyrie arrived on Sakaar she wanted to blend in. She didn't want to be recognized and reminded of her old life, so she adopted the unrefined look of a local Scrapper. Still, her warrior skills make her an exceptional bounty hunter. She's the best local in the business and demands a high price. Most of that money goes on partying, as she tries to forget all that she has lost.

One of two knives

Expensive tracker boots

Flexible leggings for athletic activity

The Grandmaster thinks Scrapper #142 is the "Best," with a capital "B." He trusts her to bring him the highest quality contenders for his Contest of Champions. That reliability earns her just about whatever she wants.

Loki and Scrapper #142 are charged by the Grandmaster with finding Hulk and Thor after they escape. Their mutual dislike quickly escalates into a fight, during which Loki spots her Asgardian tattoo. He is surprised to find that she is a Valkyrie.

DATA FILE

> Valkyrie watches Thor and Hulk's gladiator match through binoculars from her ship. She is reluctantly impressed by Thor's fighting skills.

> Valkyrie's *Warsong* is the best Scrapper ship on Sakaar. It is equipped with massive autocannons and a gyroscopic cockpit.

> After *Warsong* collides with the Grandmaster's Riot Control Ship, Valkyrie leaps from vessel to vessel, demonstrating her Asgardian super-powers and warrior training.

HONOR REGAINED

Valkyrie came to Sakaar to lose herself. Thor and Loki force her to face her past and she realizes she doesn't want to forget any more. If she must die, she'd prefer to do it killing Hela and avenging her dead sisters. Valkyrie agrees to join Thor and return to Asgard with him. To escape from Sakaar, they steal the Grandmaster's party ship, the *Commodore*. Arriving back on Asgard, she puts on an old set of Valkyrie armor and arms the ship with a cannon salvaged from an Asgardian skiff. She provides vital covering fire during the battle against Hela.

During her first encounter with Hela, Valkyrie's troop charged to meet the banished princess as she tried to escape her exile. A torrent of Hela's necroswords felled the elite warriors and their flying horses. Valkyrie was powerless as all her comrades perished.

White-gold-plated pauldron

Bulletproof silver-weave body glove

Imperial blue cape

Handlebars with squeeze trigger

Auto-lock tracer scope

Laser generation chamber

Laser focusing lens casing

Octuple barrel spindle

White-gold-plated greave

Base is bolted to the Commodore's floor

Grandmaster's favorite comfy swivel chair

SKURGE

Son of a stone mason, Skurge rises from relative obscurity to play a key role in Asgard's final days. He possesses great strength, an incredible will to survive, and is proud to have fought in Asgard's army alongside Thor. Both Loki, in disguise as Odin, and Hela place him in important jobs—guardian of the Bifrost bridge and Executioner respectively—exploiting his need for approval and submissive nature. While Skurge isn't always ethical, he realizes that there is a moral boundary he cannot cross and dies a hero.

Skurge wants recognition, but also places his own survival above anything else. He cowardly carries out Hela's evil orders without question and then hides amongst fleeing Asgardian civilians during Ragnarok. His sudden change of heart and suicidal defense of his fellow Asgardians ensures he gains fame instead of infamy.

EAGER EXECUTIONER

When Hela arrives through the Bifrost, Skurge instinctively kneels to the god of death to survive her wrath. Hela recognizes his potential and names him her Executioner. This job has fallen out of favor since Odin became a benevolent ruler, but Skurge is responsible for executing Hela's vision, and anyone she wants dead.

SKURGE'S AX

Following her father's example, Hela summons a worthy weapon for Skurge, just as Odin once gave her Mjolnir to act as his Executioner. This fearsome ax is formed from obsidian and strikes fear into his fellow Asgardians.

Faceted edges leave fearful wounds

Magically enhanced obsidian is incredibly strong

Skurge is the polar opposite of Heimdall, the former guardian of the Bifrost. The latest guardian lacks Heimdall's singular focus, and is far more interested in impressing visitors than attending to his duty of swiftly transporting them.

Skurge believes his tattoos make him even more attractive

Expensive tastes reflected in unusual color choices

Underlay armor of interlocking Uru plates

Skurge's sigil accented with rare gems

Dyed ox-leather pants

Armor forged by Dwarves

HOFUND

As guardian of the Bifrost, Skurge wields Heimdall's sword, Hofund, and is responsible for opening and closing the magical bridge. He clearly lacks the necessary respect for this iconic blade and leaves it on a pile of treasures he has found across the Nine Realms.

Strong shoulders from helping his father with masonry

SURTUR

Surtur is a giant Fire Demon who rules over the volcanic realm of Muspelheim. This long-suffering lord holds court over his fellow Fire Demon brethren and lies in wait to exact his revenge on Odin for attacking his realm.

Decorative headspikes resemble eyebrows

Teeth ground down by munching on lava bug larvae

SKURGE'S STUFF

Unlike the previous guardian of the Bifrost bridge, Skurge enjoys misusing the job's perks. He travels across the Nine Realms and steals things to make himself rich. Skurge pridefully shows his treasures to any Asgardian visitors to the Observatory, hoping to gain the approval he desperately craves.

Two of Skurge's most prized possessions are a pair of M-16 assault rifles, imaginatively named "Des" and "Troy," from Texas in Midgard. While Einherjar aren't trained to use assault rifles, Skurge proficiently wields them in battle.

Skurge is pleased to showcase his collection of wares

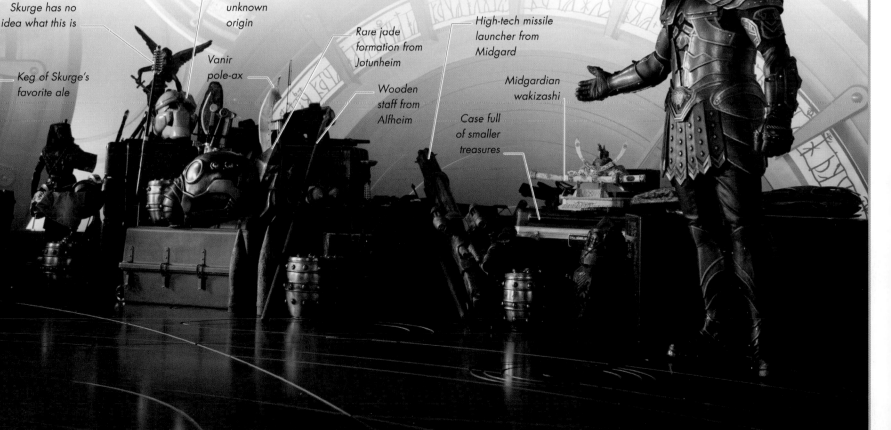

Skurge has no idea what this is

Helmet of unknown origin

Rare jade formation from Jotunheim

High-tech missile launcher from Midgard

Keg of Skurge's favorite ale

Vanir pole-ax

Wooden staff from Alfheim

Midgardian wakizashi

Case full of smaller treasures

THE AVENGERS

The universe is a very dangerous place. Powerful alien empires seek to expand across the cosmos, tyrannical rulers wage war to bring worlds under their control, and malevolent beings look with jealous eyes at the treasures that Earth has to offer. Against these, no Super Hero, no matter how powerful, can stand alone. Earth's only hope is for the mightiest heroes in the world to join forces, and fight their enemies together as a team. That team is the Avengers.

"THE AVENGERS. IT'S WHAT WE CALL OURSELVES, SORT OF LIKE A TEAM."

IRON MAN

THE AVENGERS

The Avengers is as much an idea as a team. An idea that has evolved beyond its S.H.I.E.L.D.-initiated origins as a select tactical response unit to counter unprecedented threats to humanity. It is a team whose membership adapts to the nature and level of the threat, be it homegrown, extraterrestrial, or multidimensional. When that threat is Thanos, the Mad Titan, bent on subjugating all existence, the Avengers becomes a galvanizing idea around which a diverse gathering of heroes assemble as the universe's last line of defense.

Badly damaged during the battle with Loki and his Chitauri soldiers, Stark Tower is rebuilt as Avengers Tower, a cutting-edge HQ for the Avengers. Run by JARVIS, Stark's indispensable A.I., the tower boasts state-of-the-art research labs and medical facilities, customized training equipment, a Quinjet landing pad, storage bays for Stark's Iron Legion drones, living quarters, and a stylish lounge bar.

The Avengers Initiative was a covert recruitment drive for super-powered beings proposed by S.H.I.E.L.D.'s director, Nick Fury, to fight the battles Earth's conventional forces couldn't. Shut down by the World Security Council (W.S.C.), Fury is forced to reinstate the initiative when Loki steals the alien Tesseract device from S.H.I.E.L.D.

S.H.I.E.L.D. EMBLEM

Latest stylized "global" eagle logo

EARTH'S MIGHTIEST HEROES

The Avengers had a less than promising start. A fractious and wary group brought together under the auspices of S.H.I.E.L.D. (the Strategic Homeland Intervention Enforcement and Logistics Division), they become a team forged in the heat of battle against the Asgardian Loki and his army of alien Chitauri. Led by legendary Super-Soldier Captain America, the Avenger's first roll call includes armored genius Iron Man, Asgardian demigod Thor, gamma ray-powered Hulk, super-spy Black Widow, and crack-shot archer Hawkeye. As a team, they are far more than the sum of their impressive parts, ready and able to repel any force endangering Earth.

CAPTAIN AMERICA

THOR

BLACK WIDOW

HAWKEYE

DATA FILE

> The Avengers is first identified by name when Tony Stark confronts Loki before the Chitauri invasion of New York. He also half-jokingly declares the team to be "Earth's Mightiest Heroes."

> Some time after Thor first arrives on Earth, the W.S.C. closes down the Avengers Initiative. They want S.H.I.E.L.D. to focus on "Phase 2" instead, and learn how to weaponize the Tesseract.

QUINJET

The Quinjet is an advanced personnel transport and combat vehicle. Developed by S.H.I.E.L.D. to respond to escalating global threats, the unique vertical takeoff and landing (VTOL) aircraft has turbine-powered hybrid-wings, enhanced weaponry, and retro-reflective stealth cloaking technology. Designed for maximum maneuverability, the Quinjet can make very tight turns, come to a dead stop, and hover in midair.

Cargo bay

Twin jet engines

Single pilot cockpit

GAU-17/A Gatling gun

Twin angle-adjustable rotors

The Avengers' Quinjet is a highly customized variant featuring a JARVIS-controlled autopilot system, a cargo bay for the full Avengers team, and a concealed motorcycle.

The Avengers' core members are Captain America (the strategist), Iron Man (the inventor), and Thor (the warrior). While they respect each other's abilities, their differing approaches and temperaments can sometimes spark fierce infighting, with unforeseen and far-reaching consequences.

HULK

IRON MAN

NEW AVENGERS

The Avengers' roster has changed many times over the years. Some founding members have left, while others, such as the telekinetic Scarlet Witch, the synthezoid Vision, the armored War Machine, and the winged Falcon, have joined the team's ranks. The Avengers are also a beacon for other allies, including the sorcerer Doctor Strange, the warrior-king Black Panther, the size-shifting Ant-Man, and the teen hero Spider-Man, who fight alongside them if the need arises. When Thanos seeks to wipe out half of the universe, all will heed the rallying cry: "Avengers Assemble!"

After defeating the rogue A.I. Ultron, the Avengers relocate to upstate New York. A converted Stark Industries warehouse, this new, less prominent HQ offers similar facilities to Avengers Tower, plus several support staff, including former S.H.I.E.L.D. agent Maria Hill and renowned scientists Erik Selvig and Helen Cho. The base is used for training, scientific research, and vehicle and weapons development.

NICK FURY

Former CIA agent Colonel Nicholas "Nick" Joseph Fury is Director of S.H.I.E.L.D., the government organization charged with monitoring super-beings. Fury first brings the Avengers together when the Asgardian Loki threatens Earth, and continues to monitor, advise, and assist them even after S.H.I.E.L.D. falls apart. Fury is tenaciously results-oriented. He doesn't hesitate to make hard calls or jump into battle, even when it could cost him his life or the lives of his agents. He is focused on serving not only his country, but the entire planet in the face of countless supernatural and extraterrestrial threats. He fakes his own death during the Hydra uprising and goes into hiding, though still plays a crucial role supporting the Avengers.

S.H.I.E.L.D. earpiece always linked to Deputy Director Maria Hill

Eye patch conceals scarred and non-functional left eye

Site of injury from attempted assassination

Kevlar vest

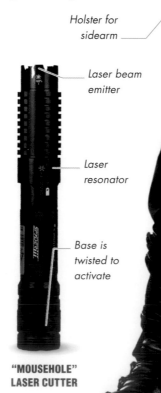

The Tesseract is an extraterrestrial cube that Fury inherits from Howard Stark, who recovered it from the North Atlantic. By testing the object as a potential source of energy, S.H.I.E.L.D. unwittingly sows the seeds for Loki's invasion of Earth.

S.H.I.E.L.D. DIRECTOR

Fury is the Director of the Strategic Homeland Intervention Enforcement and Logistics Division (S.H.I.E.L.D.), managing a number of projects that serve the security interests of the U.S. and its allies. Foremost of these is the so-called Avengers Initiative: the countering of threats to Earth by means of an elite team of super-powered beings. Most concerned with extraterrestrial dangers, Fury focuses on developing weapons technology to combat them while utilizing the Avengers for defense.

Holster for sidearm

Energy siphon channels

TESSERACT ACCELERATOR

Tesseract containment field

Laser beam emitter

Laser resonator

Base is twisted to activate

Boot contains hidden knife

"MOUSEHOLE" LASER CUTTER

S.H.I.E.L.D.-issue boots contain security microchips for accessing restricted areas

DATA FILE

> Fury is a tactical genius, skilled in military techniques including deception and evasion.

> A skilled pilot, Fury has experience flying helicopters and S.H.I.E.L.D. Quinjets.

> Fury often makes jokes about his eye to ease the tension in stressful situations.

Nick Fury is taken by surprise when Hydra rises up from within the ranks of S.H.I.E.L.D. and tries to assassinate him. He had put his trust in the organization's leadership, unaware that the only ones he could really count on were subordinates like Captain America and Black Widow.

It is up to Nick Fury alone to decide who can join the Avengers Initiative, and he personally recruits those he believes worthy. As billionaire genius Tony Stark discovers, simply having super-powers or access to advanced technology is by no means a guarantee of acceptance. Fury's criteria are extremely strict.

Even when Fury is no longer director of S.H.I.E.L.D. or actively overseeing the Avengers, he monitors them and steps in when they need him most. He shows up at just the right time when they retreat to Hawkeye's farm during Ultron's offensive.

Nick Fury feels at home on the Helicarrier's bridge, choosing it as his HQ during major battles in New York and Sokovia. He won't tolerate anyone who questions his command, sometimes shooting down pilots who disobey his orders.

HELICARRIER

S.H.I.E.L.D.'s flagship is a flying command center and launching platform known as the Helicarrier. Designed in part with technology created by Howard Stark, it uses four large turbine engines to fly at altitudes of up to 30,000 ft (9,140 m). The ship is massive in size, yet remains hidden from most of the population thanks to holographic stealth technology that obscures its hull when viewed from below. It carries a large contingent of Quinjets, F-35 Lightning II fighter jets, and helicopters ready for deployment.

The Helicarrier is fully submersible and seaworthy, and is a maneuverable aircraft, too. Tony Stark upgrades its engines with his own repulsor technology following the Battle of New York, making it capable of flying indefinitely.

Bridge (command, navigation, and communications)

Angled rear flight deck for landings

Aircraft elevator to hangar

Forward flight deck for takeoffs

Crew accommodation in bow section

Lift rotor (one of four)

PHIL COULSON

Agent Phillip J. Coulson is one of S.H.I.E.L.D. Director Nick Fury's top operatives, and a dedicated career agent. His amiable, humble approach endears him to both his S.H.I.E.L.D. colleagues and the civilians he meets. However, sometimes he intermingles personal and professional life more than a S.H.I.E.L.D. agent should, and so inadvertently erodes his own image as an authority figure. Coulson assists Fury in the recruitment of all the original Avengers and their assimilation into the team. He is killed by Loki when the Asgardian escapes from confinement aboard the S.H.I.E.L.D. Helicarrier.

Coulson is very excited when he meets Captain America for the first time, as Coulson is a longtime Cap fan—he actually helped redesign Cap's suit. He also has ten Captain America cards in near-mint condition that he hopes Cap will sign.

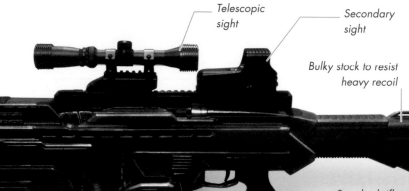

S.H.I.E.L.D. earpiece

Original Destroyer armor plating

Telescopic sight

Secondary sight

Bulky stock to resist heavy recoil

Standard rifle grip

DESTROYER CANNON
This powerful weapon is a prototype fashioned from the remains of the Asgardian automaton known as the Destroyer. It is kept in a secure locker requiring a retinal scan. Coulson uses it to battle Loki, but admits he has no idea what it will do until he fires it for the first time.

S.H.I.E.L.D. AGENT
Phil Coulson is a seasoned S.H.I.E.L.D. agent. His first brush with a prospective Avenger occurs when Tony Stark returns home from Afghanistan. S.H.I.E.L.D. is interested in Stark's new armor technology, so Coulson is sent to interview him. Coulson is good at screening potential Avengers for his boss—something he does in the case of both Tony Stark and Thor. This, combined with experience working in the field with fellow agents Black Widow and Hawkeye, makes him ideally suited to bringing the Avengers Initiative to fruition.

Analog watch—a gift from a long-lost friend

Coulson is Fury's right-hand man. Fury likes him and so do the Avengers. When Coulson is killed, Fury uses his death to motivate the Avengers to stick together and stop Loki.

DATA FILE

> Coulson first encounters Thor when he is sent to investigate the New Mexico crash site of Thor's hammer, Mjolnir.

> Coulson has a temporary S.H.I.E.L.D. facility built around Mjolnir because it is impossible to move it.

> Assuming that Earth names work the same way as Asgardian ones, Thor calls Coulson "Son of Coul."

MARIA HILL

Maria Hill is the deputy director of S.H.I.E.L.D. and trusted confidant of Nick Fury. She is a no-nonsense, by-the-book agent—which sometimes puts her at odds with Fury's more flexible approach. Maria may question his orders, but only as a point of providing him with alternatives. She is committed to her boss and remains loyal to Fury when others around him lose faith. Even after S.H.I.E.L.D. self-destructs, Hill remains in close contact with Fury, acting as a covert liaison between him and the Avengers.

Tracking device hidden in sleeve

Adapter for form-fitting ear insert

Processor and battery module

Antenna with microphone tip

ENCRYPTED EARPIECE
Hill's S.H.I.E.L.D.-issue earpiece was developed by Stark Industries. A tap on the processor module toggles between preset communication channels.

Fire-resistant S.H.I.E.L.D. jumpsuit

Glock 19 pistol in adjustable holster

Maria Hill feels most at home in the command center on board the S.H.I.E.L.D. Helicarrier. There, she coordinates the capture and confinement of Loki and the subsequent Battle of New York.

Maria Hill is on good terms with all the Avengers, though she does like to tease them. She spends time with them socially outside of work and is present at the party in Avengers Tower where Ultron gains sentience.

DEPUTY DIRECTOR

As Nick Fury's second-in-command, Hill has a high level of responsibility. It's her job to foresee possible problems and provide feedback to Fury. Her agency-minded methods mean they don't always see eye to eye, but she always follows his orders. When Fury fakes his death, Hill is the only person that he trusts to know the entire truth. However, the situation leaves her bearing the full weight of the government's accusations when S.H.I.E.L.D. unravels, requiring Hill to seek legal protection from within Stark Industries.

CRACK SHOT
Steady of eye and hand, Hill possesses marksmanship skills that are legendary. She is especially noted for her ability to hit targets with extreme accuracy, even when both she and they are moving.

Two-handed grip for accuracy

After S.H.I.E.L.D. is destroyed from within by Hydra, Hill applies for employment at Stark Industries. She uses Stark's resources to monitor security situations and sends Nick Fury regular updates. Hill also provides support for the Avengers' mission to retrieve Loki's scepter from Hydra's base in Sokovia.

Boots conceal a compact weapon

HULK

Bruce Banner, MD, PhD is a brilliant, yet pleasantly modest scientist. He is thrown into a turbulent new life when the U.S. military recruits him into a program that—unbeknownst to him—is trying to recreate the Super-Soldier Serum that produced Captain America. Dosed with gamma rays in an experiment gone wrong, Bruce now sporadically transforms into a raging green monster with terrifying strength, dubbed "Hulk."

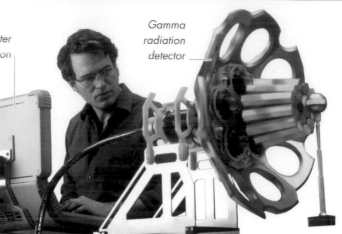

Computer workstation

Gamma radiation detector

Shaggy, unkempt hair

DR. BANNER

Bruce Banner has seven PhDs, in nuclear physics, radiophysics, biochemistry, engineering, robotics, computer science, and mathematics. He generally appears calm and mild-mannered, with a quirky sense of humor—in stark contrast to his alter ego, Hulk. Banner tries to hide from the world, until S.H.I.E.L.D. drags him back into conflict.

SMARTEST MAN

Banner is the brains of the Avengers—S.H.I.E.L.D. agent Phil Coulson compares him to Professor Stephen Hawking. Banner is more methodical and less impulsive than Tony Stark, and collaborates with Stark on his greatest inventions.

BECOMING A MONSTER

Bruce Banner's transformations are triggered by negative feelings: frustration, anxiety, worry, fear, pain, and above all, anger. Banner is always a little angry on some level, but he learns to manage it and harness it when needed. Hulk's transformation back into Banner requires feelings at the opposite end of the spectrum: calmness, serenity, and love.

Head pulled back in pain

Expanding chest bursting through shirt

Service ribbons

GENERAL ROSS

Thaddeus E. "Thunderbolt" Ross manages the U.S. Army's Bio-Tech Force Enhancement Project, the unit charged with recreating Dr. Erskine's Super-Soldier Serum. He is responsible for recruiting Bruce Banner to the program. Ross' professional obsessions later put him at odds with the Avengers—as Secretary of State, he ruthlessly oversees the Sokovia Accords.

Ross is willing to do anything to stop the Hulk. He collects a sample of the Super-Soldier Serum to inject into Royal Marine Emil Blonsky, creating Hulk's nemesis—a monster known as Abomination.

Thick skull

Bulletproof skin and near unbreakable bones

Face is a large, green, distorted version of Banner's

HULK SMASH

Hulk, or "the other guy" as Banner calls him, has only one interest: venting rage through violence. This involves smashing buildings, hurling vehicles, pummeling monsters, and causing general mayhem. This is his most valuable asset—and perhaps the only useful one—to the Avengers. His smashing skills aid them in battles against the alien Chitauri, a resurgent Hydra, and the android Ultron. Turning the Hulk off—reverting him to Bruce Banner—is difficult, and increasingly so with each transformation.

Muscles bigger than an average man's waist

Hawkeye and the Avengers are uneasy about working with the Hulk during the Chitauri invasion of Earth. However, having an aggressive target like the Chitauri helps keep Hulk more focused and less dangerous to civilians.

Powerful legs can leap hundreds of feet

At first, S.H.I.E.L.D. and the Avengers fear rousing the Hulk, aware that his incredible strength makes him a living weapon of mass destruction. Over time, though, they learn how to use his powers to best effect.

DATA FILE

> Banner was a professor of biochemistry and radiophysics at Culver University and a colleague of renowned scientist Dr. Erik Selvig.

> While Banner is in hiding, S.H.I.E.L.D. tracks Hulk via ten "Gamma Incidents" from Idaho to Paraguay, though Black Widow finally locates him in India.

Feet can stomp holes through cement

HULK: LOSING CONTROL

Bruce Banner has always been afraid of the destructive power of the Hulk, but he learns to channel it for good as an Avenger… that is, until events in Johannesburg, when Hulk's rampage destroys a large portion of the city. His actions begin to turn the world against the Avengers. After aiding in the defeat of the deranged A.I. Ultron, Hulk leaves Earth's troubles behind and looks for a place in the cosmos where he can smash in peace.

Though Tony Stark shoulders all of the blame and bitter consequences, Banner shares responsibility in the creation of Ultron. The two collaborate on many projects, but none of the others turn out so badly.

Natasha Romanoff (Black Widow) and Bruce Banner share a mutual attraction. Both Avengers feel isolated from society due to who they've become. Natasha thinks this makes them a good match, but Bruce fears he will disappoint her.

DUEL IN JOHANNESBURG

While she is still aiding Ultron, Scarlet Witch uses her abilities on Banner, transforming him into the rampaging Hulk. In an effort to subdue him, Tony Stark calls on his satellite platform, Veronica, to deliver the "Hulkbuster" (Mark XLIV) armor. This tank-sized suit was designed by Stark and Banner together.

The battle between Hulk and Hulkbuster leaves parts of the city in ruins. The Hulk only stops when he is completely worn down and knocked out.

Emergency access hatch

Sleeping gas canisters

Hulk is irritated and tired

CALMING THE HULK

Natasha and Banner have developed a routine to calm the Hulk down. Natasha says "Hey big guy. Sun's getting real low." Then she raises her palm, facing him. Next, Hulk presses his against hers. Finally, she holds her palm facing up, with his hand placed on top, and she runs her hand below and above his.

Arm held down, submissively

A simple series of caresses from Natasha soothes the savage Hulk, transforming him back into Banner.

Palm extended forward in conciliation

Hulk enjoys his newfound popularity on Sakaar. He knows that his destructive tendencies made him unpopular on Earth and is in no hurry to return. He doesn't really want to kill Thor, but he also doesn't want Thor to ruin things for him.

Hammer is repurposed engine part

Crest makes already huge Hulk appear gigantic

Decorative teeth stamped in hammer

CHAMPION OF SAKAAR

After throwing Ultron out of a Quinjet in Sokovia, Hulk flies off into space, and is eventually funneled to the planet Sakaar by a wormhole. There, he becomes the new reigning champion in Sakaar's brutal gladiatorial games. After spending two whole years as Hulk, with no moderating influence from Banner, he doesn't hesitate to smash Thor when he meets his former ally in the arena.

Blade pierces exoskeletons and armor

Pauldron made from salvaged ship hull

Crest of winged horse hair

HULK'S ARENA HELMET

Extension protects Hulk's jaw

Flame symbol of a "smashed" former adversary

OPPONENT'S SHIELD (KEPT AS TROPHY)

DATA FILE

> Hulk is a confident warrior. He isn't afraid of losing. His only real fear is reverting into "weak and puny" Bruce Banner.

> Hulk tries to forget Black Widow, but seeing a video of her on the Quinjet makes him heartsick and transforms him back into Banner.

Custom-fitted greaves protect Hulk's shins

After their battle, Thor and Hulk reconnect and bond on Sakaar. Hulk may act like he doesn't care whether Thor stays or goes, but deep down he is lonely and enjoys their new camaraderie.

Sandal soles made from Quinjet tires

BLACK WIDOW

Natasha Romanoff was once a member of the KGB—the Soviet Union's secret intelligence service—and a top Russian spy, code-named Black Widow. She posed such a threat to U.S. national security that S.H.I.E.L.D. agent Clint Barton was ordered to eliminate her. However, realizing that her skill as an assassin made her a potential asset, he instead recruited her to S.H.I.E.L.D., and later, the Avengers.

THE RED ROOM

Young Natasha Romanoff took part in the KGB's secret "Red Room" spy training program, emerging with a finely honed physique and a mind unrivaled in its steeliness. Natasha became one of the world's most ruthless spies and assassins whose code name—that of a deadly spider—is well deserved.

"NATALIE RUSHMAN"

As a S.H.I.E.L.D. agent, Black Widow is assigned to infiltrate Stark Industries and evaluate whether Tony Stark is a suitable candidate for the Avengers Initiative. She is hired under the identity of "Natalie Rushman" for Stark's Legal Department. When Pepper Potts is promoted to Stark Industries CEO, Black Widow gets close to Stark by becoming his new personal assistant.

When Black Widow infiltrates Hammer Industries to capture the rogue physicist Ivan Vanko, she subdues a dozen security guards in under a minute.

S.H.I.E.L.D. AGENT

Black Widow's missions fall into two main categories: infiltration and combat. For the former, she forgoes her high-tech gear and weaponry and wears simple clothing in order to better blend in with her targets.

Leather jacket worn open and casual

Left hand ready to draw sidearm

Sturdy boots

S.H.I.E.L.D. symbol on shoulders

One of two Glock 26 pistols

BATTLE OF NEW YORK

As a member of the newly formed Avengers and still a S.H.I.E.L.D. agent, Natasha must enter a chaotic urban war zone in New York. Her utilitarian uniform is designed for a variety of duties—but most of all, heavy combat.

Reinforced toe caps for powerful kicks

Smooth fabric offers enemies little handhold in close combat

LAST DAYS OF S.H.I.E.L.D.

Working with S.H.I.E.L.D.'s elite STRIKE team shortly before the organization's collapse, Black Widow adopts a new uniform. Sleek and stealthy, it is designed for nighttime black-ops missions.

Red hourglass Black Widow symbol

Widow's Bite weapon

Pistols give option to use lethal force

Wedge heels

While Black Widow's formidable combat skills make her a force to be reckoned with, she frequently does not have to use them. She is adept at infiltrating organizations and manipulating her targets into divulging secret information.

LETHAL SKILLS

Black Widow is one of the most dangerous people in the world. Her unrivaled knowledge of martial arts is combined with acrobatic and gymnastic skills that exceed those of the best Olympic-level athletes. She easily disarms and defeats targets far larger or stronger than herself.

VEHICULAR COMBAT

Black Widow's off-road driving and acrobatic abilities allow her to accomplish incredible feats, such as dodging obstacles and enemy attacks at high speed, while simultaneously firing her weapons.

Flawless balance

DATA FILE

> Black Widow speaks many languages, including Russian, English, French, Vietnamese, Italian, Mandarin, and Latin.

> A skilled and experienced pilot, Black Widow is able to take the controls of almost any aircraft with complete confidence.

FAST AND ACCURATE

Her "Red Room" training allows Black Widow to hit enemy targets quickly and at great distances. She is an expert markswoman, even with adapted alien technology such as Hydra's energy blasters.

Calm and focused expression

Electric "Widow Stings" defense system courses through suit

Suit charger packs

Widow's Bite control interface

Upgraded Widow's Bite

Insulated gauntlets

Kevlar and stretchable fabric mix

Electroshock batons

Kneepad delivers powerful external shock on impact

Boots insulated to prevent shocks

Magnetic rails stabilize bolt

Hybrid Chitauri-Hydra weapon

Energy cell

SOKOVIA UNIFORM

BLACK WIDOW: DIVIDED LOYALTIES

Black Widow's Russian family are dead, S.H.I.E.L.D. is gone, and her friend Bruce Banner has disappeared. Her Avengers teammates are her only family now, so it is heartbreaking for Natasha to watch them split apart over the Sokovia Accords and the hunt for Bucky Barnes. She strives to hold them together as long as she can, but in the end, Natasha is forced to turn away and become a fugitive herself.

The Widow's Bite is one of Black Widow's most powerful weapons. Developed by S.H.I.E.L.D., it is an electroshock weapon contained in her gauntlets. Its blast is strong enough to subdue even Black Panther.

Retractable electroshock wand

Magnetic grip handle

Custom-tailored Kevlar jumpsuit

Widow's Bite gauntlet with long-range upgrade

Black Widow symbol

Utility belt with brass buckle

Steve Rogers and Natasha share a bond after their time spent on the run together during the Hydra uprising. Natasha comforts her friend after Peggy Carter's London funeral.

STUCK IN THE MIDDLE

Natasha believes it is vital for the Avengers to stick together, both as friends and as a team. The idea of choosing sides causes her great anguish. Signing the Sokovia Accords could mean saving the Avengers. However, it would also mean siding with Stark—and the last thing she wants is to help Stark condemn her friend Steve Rogers and Barnes, who she believes is innocent of the crimes he is accused of. Natasha feels she is in an impossible position.

On the Avengers operation in Lagos, Black Widow must keep a lookout in the market for Crossbones and his men, who plan to steal biological weapons. As usual, her skills at going incognito stand her in good stead.

Stretchable bulletproof fabric

Flexible knee armor

Internal titanium shin armor plating

Unused holster strap

MEETING T'CHALLA

Black Widow's spy training also makes her an effective diplomat. Natasha attends the signing of the Sokovia Accords in Vienna as the Avengers' official representative. There, she meets Prince T'Challa of Wakanda and expresses her sorrow for the loss of 11 of his people in the Lagos attack.

Tense posture—Western politics makes T'Challa feel on edge

Official diplomatic attire

Kinetic rebounding soles add bounce to jumps

The atmosphere is tense in the Joint Counter Terrorist Center in Berlin, as Natasha, the other Avengers, and Agent Sharon Carter wait for Barnes, a.k.a. the Winter Soldier, to be evaluated. At this point, the Avengers' loyalties to each other are severely strained; shortly afterward, the team collapses into conflict.

Natasha hoped to resolve the Avengers' internal conflict peacefully by talking Cap and his team into surrendering. When some of the less experienced Avengers escalate the violence, Natasha can only look on in despair.

DATA FILE

> Stark asks Natasha if she can get Hulk to help them in the Avengers Civil War, but she says she doesn't think he would be on their side.

> Natasha recruits Black Panther to Stark's team, hoping this will keep Black Panther accountable and prevent him from killing the Winter Soldier or Steve Rogers.

> After helping Cap and the Winter Soldier escape from Leipzig-Halle Airport, Natasha goes on the run.

HAWKEYE

S.H.I.E.L.D. Agent Clint Barton (code name: Hawkeye) is an incredible marksman and long-time member of the Avengers. His links to the Avengers Initiative begin with Thor—he is assigned to security at the New Mexico crash site of Thor's hammer, Mjolnir. When Thor's brother, Loki, attempts to conquer Earth, the Asgardian god of mischief brainwashes Hawkeye, setting him against S.H.I.E.L.D. and the Avengers. Hawkeye causes mayhem, but eventually is freed from Loki's control, allowing him to join the Avengers for the crucial Battle of New York. He goes on to play a key role in the battle against the android Ultron, before retiring—albeit only briefly.

During the Battle of Sokovia, Hawkeye and Scarlet Witch work together to evacuate civilians while fighting off Ultron's drones.

Dual compartments

Next arrow is ready to grab

WAR IN SOKOVIA

Hawkeye's next mission is to Sokovia, where the Avengers try to destroy Hydra once and for all. For this operation, Hawkeye upgrades to a new bow and clothing more suitable to a chilly climate. He is wounded in action, but returns to Sokovia to face Ultron after the megalomaniacal android takes over the country.

SOKOVIA QUIVER

At the start of Loki's invasion, Hawkeye is head of security for S.H.I.E.L.D.'s Tesseract project. When the Tesseract begins emitting unusual radiation, Hawkeye notifies Nick Fury, but is powerless when Loki appears from a portal and seizes control of his mind.

Bowstring held under tension

Sight

Arrow rest

Anchor point (string is drawn back to chin)

Family photo tucked inside tunic

MASTER BOWMAN

Hawkeye's astonishing reflexes make him uniquely suited to his weapon of choice—bows. He has a huge collection of them, and always matches the bow to the mission; in the Battle of New York, he uses a collapsible recurve bow with a laser sight. All have remote controls for electronic quivers that prepare his trick arrowheads. These arrowheads include rappelling lines, electronic jamming devices, EMPs, timed explosives, and flash arrowheads.

Shooting glove

Jacket for cold Sokovian weather

Site of Hydra -inflicted injury

Elastic collar

Bulletproof vest

Bracer (arm guard)

Carbon fiber bow limb

In New York, Hawkeye takes a high vantage point atop a building across from Stark Tower. His job is to act as lookout and shoot down Chitauri chariots with explosive arrows.

BATTLE OF NEW YORK EQUIPMENT

Unknown to all but a select few—and uniquely for an Avenger—Barton has a wife and children. They live in an idyllic old farmhouse, which isn't listed in any of S.H.I.E.L.D.'s records. This makes it a great place for the Avengers to hide out after the Hulk destroys parts of Johannesburg.

Outfit has 145 separate pattern pieces

Straps for optional knife or ankle holster

BATTLE OF SOKOVIA EQUIPMENT

Hawkeye joins the Avengers Civil War on Cap's side; this time armed with a bow that folds into a melee weapon. He doesn't want to actually hurt any of his friends, though, and Scarlet Witch accuses him of pulling his punches.

DATA FILE

> Hawkeye is a left-handed bowman, meaning he holds the bow with his right hand and draws the string with his left.

> Black Widow and Hawkeye are close, having fought together as S.H.I.E.L.D. agents many times. Of the Avengers, only she knew that Hawkeye had a family.

Arrows locked securely in quiver

Hybrid aluminum/ carbon arrow shafts

Shafts remain stationary as heads rotate

OUT OF RETIREMENT

Hawkeye struggles between commitment to the Avengers and devotion to his family. After Ultron's defeat, Barton decides to retire and spend more time at home, but is pulled back into combat when Cap asks for his help to oppose Tony Stark. Barton liberates fellow Avenger Wanda Maximoff from her Stark-inflicted house arrest, in part because he feels indebted to her brother for sacrificing himself in Sokovia. He fights beside her and Cap in the Avengers face-off at Leipzig-Halle Airport, but is captured, and ends up in the Raft prison—until he is broken out by Cap.

Highly attuned eyesight

Auto-adjusted quiver shoulder strap

Recurve bow—offers more power than compound bow, but harder to use

Bowstring nocking point

Gauntlet vibrates when its sensors detect muscle strain

LEIPZIG-HALLE QUIVER

Rotating arrowhead carousel

S.H.I.E.L.D.-issue boots

Bow folding point

Electrified arrowhead

CHITAURI

The Chitauri are a hideous alien race of cyborg soldiers who share a hive mind. Thanos provides the Asgardian prince Loki with a Chitauri army for his invasion of Earth—an invasion that results in the destructive Battle of New York. Though they are extremely powerful, the Chitauri have a weakness: when the Chitauri Mothership is destroyed by the Avengers, the hive's connection with the Chitauri on Earth is broken and all of them perish. The wreckage of their weapons then falls into the hands of criminals and terrorists.

MOTHERSHIP

The Chitauri Mothership is large, slow, and vulnerable, so it remains beyond the wormhole to Earth and outside the battlefield. This ship is vital to the war. It not only coordinates Chitauri battle tactics, it controls soldiers directly via their implants.

Melee blade

Hand is inserted here

Charged particle field

Inert surface plating

Rifle barrel

Charge amplification chamber

INFANTRY CANNON

Detonator core

Hardened skull plate

Sensory nodule

Plates fused to body as exoskeleton

Activation indicator lights

Dual thumbs

Particle destabilizers

GRENADE

Trigger

CHITAURI INFANTRY

The Chitauri are a cold-blooded, technologically advanced race. They are born as fully organic beings, but their soldiers are cybernetically enhanced at an early age with electronic neural networks and armor fused to their bodies. Infantry are dependent upon chemical stimulants to enhance their strength and agility and internal reactors to power their cybernetic implants.

LONG-RANGE RIFLE

Eye holes
through dense
armor plating

Toothy maw

Antigravity
tech in flipper

LEVIATHANS

The Chitauri arrive on Earth aboard enormous flying creatures called Leviathans. Like the Chitauri infantry themselves, these beasts are cybernetically augmented. They have antigravity systems allowing them to fly in Earth's atmosphere and massive armor plates grafted to their bodies. Squads of Chitauri infantry ride into battle inside compartments under the Leviathans' scales.

DATA FILE

> A monument honoring the civilian casualties of the Battle of New York is later built in New York City.

> When Wanda Maximoff uses her powers to show Tony Stark his worst fear, she gives him a terrifying vision of an even greater war against the Chitauri, to be fought at some point in the future.

BATTLE OF NEW YORK

The Chitauri invasion and resulting Battle of New York is a defining moment for the Avengers. They are faced with an unimaginable situation—a full-scale alien invasion of the largest city in the United States, combined with a nuclear missile strike launched by a panicking World Security Council. Though the Avengers are ultimately victorious, the battle leaves deep scars, not just on the city, but the entire world, and also on the Avengers themselves.

Cap protects
his body by
kneeling behind
his shield

The Chitauri are not expecting to face super-powered humans. Loki convinced their military leaders that humanity was weak and would be easily subjugated.

A PUBLIC VICTORY

The Battle of New York suddenly thrusts the Avengers into the public eye. There is much gratitude for their role in saving the planet, but also widespread fear of the new world of aliens and super-powered warriors that the battle foreshadows.

WAR ON HYDRA

When S.H.I.E.L.D. falls, the Hydra infrastructure embedded within it, led by Baron Strucker, flees to a secret facility inside a Sokovian castle. There, Hydra develops new weapons based on Chitauri equipment salvaged from the Battle of New York. The alien technology provides a tremendous source of power, lethal energy weapons, and resilient building materials. Hydra must prepare for an imminent battle with the Avengers, who are hunting down all of Hydra's remaining cells around the globe.

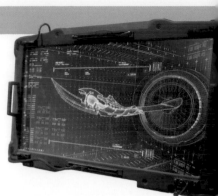

Hydra scientists work in the basement of Strucker's castle, re-engineering Chitauri equipment. A Leviathan corpse hangs from the ceiling while damaged Chitauri energy weapons, armor, and chariot propulsion modules are strewn across laboratory tables.

Monocle with augmented reality overlay

Austere uniform

BARON STRUCKER

Wolfgang von Strucker is a leading Hydra operative and former scientific mind within S.H.I.E.L.D. A highly intelligent engineer, scientist, and military strategist, he has secret dealings with some of the world's most infamous terrorists and underworld players. In addition to Chitauri technology, he steals Loki's scepter and uses it to conduct experiments on human subjects. The Maximoff twins are the only survivors of this program. Although the Avengers capture Strucker alive, he is subsequently killed in his cell by the rogue android Ultron.

DR. LIST

Dr. List was already working on secret research at Strucker's Sokovian castle when S.H.I.E.L.D. collapsed. His first project used Loki's scepter to power experimental weaponry. Next, he executes Strucker's plan to use the scepter's power on human subjects.

Tense posture due to fear of imminent defeat

HYDRA INFANTRY

Hydra's elite soldiers wear exo-suits that blend Arctic military uniforms with Chitauri technology. The suits amplify their strength and protect their bodies, while energy dischargers on each fist are controlled by a neural interface. Their rifles fire bolts of Chitauri energy rather than bullets; Strucker's engineers are only beginning to unlock the potential of the Chitauri tech when the Avengers intervene.

The Avengers infiltrate the snowy forests surrounding Hydra's Sokovian base. They must deal with both futuristic Hydra weapons and conventional artillery, as well as Pietro Maximoff speeding through the forest unseen.

Hydra's weapons are conventional machines and firearms that have been augmented with alien tech. Strucker's engineers take Cold War-era artillery and upgrade it to create devastating anti-aircraft batteries.

Cyborg implants enhance dexterity

Packs carry Chitauri power sources

Lens has internal heads-up display

Communications interface

COMBAT HELMET

Powered exoskeleton

Fist energy-braces pack charged punches

Mechanical reinforced joints

Hamstring brace

Selectively magnetic boots

Collapsible stock

Magnetic rails stabilize energy bolts

HYDRA H3L-A ENERGY RIFLE

Replaceable energy module

Wide double-barreled cannon

Reactive armor plating

Advanced custom-built turret

Gunner's periscope

HYDRA TANK

Hydra's hybrid tanks are Russian-made BMP armored fighting vehicles, upgraded with armor panels, sensor arrays, EMP emitters, and powerful Chitauri pulse weapons. The interior comfortably fits a dozen soldiers.

SCARLET WITCH

Wanda Maximoff's uncanny, magic-like abilities such as telekinesis earn her the moniker of "Scarlet Witch." Once a sworn enemy of the Avengers, Wanda joins the team during the fight against Ultron. Life never runs smoothly for Wanda: She is still discovering the extent of her powers, which continue to grow, and at times she struggles to control them. The public fears her abilities, which leaves Wanda feeling low and isolated—never more so than when she is partly responsible for a tragic accident. Despite these setbacks, resilient Wanda picks herself back up every time her team needs her help.

Born in Sokovia, Wanda and Pietro Maximoff are twins, with Pietro the elder by 12 minutes. They volunteer for a life-changing experiment at Baron Strucker's Hydra facility, where Loki's stolen scepter is used to give them extraordinary powers.

Wanda's powers are modulated by emotion. When she senses the death of her brother during the battle against Ultron, the anguish causes her powers to overload, vaporizing the swarming Ultron sentries and disassembling everything around her.

DATA FILE

> Disgruntled Sokovians create graffiti to protest the use of Stark Industries weapons in their ruinous civil wars.

> After Ultron's defeat, many Sokovians blame the Avengers for the destruction of their city, rather than Ultron.

Waves of telekinetic energy

Fingers ripple in twirling movements

Leather jacket over corset-style blouse

Flexible material for wide range of motion

Sokovian-style knee-high leather boots

"SHE'S WEIRD"

She may be called Scarlet Witch, but Wanda's powers aren't derived from the occult. Whether it altered her or merely unlocked something latent inside Wanda, the Infinity Stone in Loki's scepter bestowed incredible powers of the mind. Wanda's internal neuro-electric interface allows her to conjure blasts of red telekinetic energy. She can also use this energy to create barriers, levitate, and move objects; to communicate and read thoughts by telepathy; and even to manipulate the minds of others.

Unsuspecting Iron Man tries to dodge falling hazards

TROUBLE IN LAGOS

In the midst of a battle with the mercenary Crossbones in Lagos, Nigeria, Wanda saves Cap by pushing a bomb blast up into the sky. Unfortunately, she inadvertently hits a building with it and kills 26 people, including 11 Wakandan aid workers. This tragedy becomes the catalyst for the Avengers' Civil War.

Wanda is still young and has yet to fully master her powers. After the Lagos disaster, Vision and Tony Stark try to prevent further incidents by confining her to the Avengers facility. Despite the compound's many distractions, she feels very alone and dislikes being restricted.

During the battle between the Avengers at Leipzig-Halle Airport, Scarlet Witch creatively makes use of her surroundings by pulling cars out of the parking garage with her powers. They plunge toward Iron Man, who ends up at the bottom of a pile. Unlike the other Avengers, Wanda isn't pulling any punches.

Wanda's sweeping arm gestures drag vehicles out through the wall

During the battle in Sokovia, Pietro is nearly exhausted by the sheer physical exertion required to save so many civilians. He is eventually killed trying to shield Hawkeye and a Sokovian child. Hawkeye names his own son Nathaniel Pietro Barton to honor the Sokovian's memory.

QUICKSILVER

Pietro has a tough time adjusting to his new abilities. With practice, however, plus his accelerated metabolism and more efficient organs, he is able to sustain incredible velocities, earning him the name "Quicksilver." His rage also helps drive him—the twins were orphaned at just ten years old, when bombs labeled "Stark Industries" destroyed their Sokovian home. The twins align with Hydra, and then Ultron in hopes of getting revenge against Stark, though both have a change of heart when they discover the android's plan to wipe out humanity.

Tensions run high between Pietro and Hawkeye as they keep seeking to best each other and exchange taunts about slow reactions. Their strained relationship doesn't mellow until they work together during battle.

Gloves keep sleeves from flying up

ULTRON

Ultron is an evil sentient android, inadvertently created by Tony Stark while Stark is trying to develop an A.I. to manage a new global peacekeeping system. Upon completion, Ultron suddenly becomes self-aware and aggressively hostile. He quickly assimilates vast amounts of digital data and knowledge of world history and cultures. At his core, though, Ultron is self-absorbed and immature. This imbalance of child-like emotions and vast intellect, mixed with an obsession with saving the world from humanity—a distortion of his original peacekeeping program—endows Ultron with apocalyptic ambitions.

- Leviathan anti-gravity device in palms
- Holographic memory system
- Reactor glow visible
- Reactor core and central processor
- Electrical relays and fluid systems
- Knee mechanics copied from Hydra Exo-suit
- Shin brace and ankle actuator
- Chitauri prosthetic foot design

Bruce Banner and Tony Stark compare Stark's JARVIS A.I. (left) and the alien code inside Loki's scepter (right). Both show non-human minds, but the alien code appears to process thoughts much like an organic, living brain. Stark sees a template to develop Ultron.

Ultron first emerges in a temporary body, hobbled together out of damaged parts from Iron Legion drones (Stark's A.I.-controlled, drone suits that support the Avengers on missions). Ultron stumbles into a party at Avengers Tower, and launches an attack to test the Avengers' mettle, before transferring his consciousness via the internet to the Eastern European city state of Sokovia.

In Sokovia, Ultron builds an impressive new body for himself using the alien Chitauri tech salvaged by Hydra. This body gives him super-human strength and durability, and the power to manipulate gravity and fire beams of glowing red plasma from his fingertips.

STARK'S NEMESIS

Once Ultron is conscious, he hears Tony Stark's name and immediately searches all available data on the internet to discover who Stark is. Ultron learns about the Avengers, Stark Industries' weapons programs, and Tony Stark's efforts to bring about peace using technology. He sees Stark as a hypocrite and deeply resents being compared to him—or reminded that Stark is his creator. Ultron views Stark and the Avengers as the biggest threat to Earth and endeavors to destroy them all.

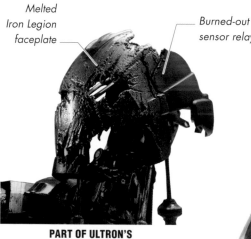

- Melted Iron Legion faceplate
- Burned-out sensor relays

PART OF ULTRON'S FIRST BODY

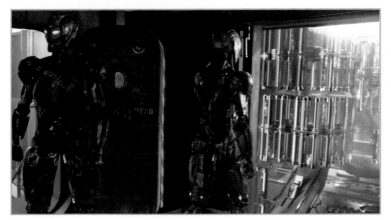

Ultron needs vast quantities of rare vibranium metal, both to build another replacement body and to construct his doomsday device. Ultron and the Maximoff twins travel to South Africa, where they take it from the embittered arms dealer Ulysses Klaue.

Light armor is easy to produce

"Ears" are transmitter and receiver antennae

Limbs are modular and easily upgraded

Modified repulsor tech in torso

BATTLE OF SOKOVIA

Ultron plans to wipe out humanity and populate the Earth with machines that he will control. He intends to achieve this by lifting Sokovia into the air with a giant device based on vibranium and Chitauri technology, and then dropping it like a meteor onto the Earth's surface. Ultron knows the Avengers will try to stop him, so he creates a huge army of expendable sentries. He hopes that the Avengers will be so preoccupied with fighting them and trying to save Sokovia's civilians that they will miss the larger threat.

ULTRON SENTRIES

Ultron's sentries are based on Tony Stark's Iron Legion drones. Though individually weak, they can be quickly mass-produced, providing Ultron with a large army. He can take personal control of any sentry—when this happens its eyes turn red.

Vibranium detonator

DOOMSDAY TRIGGER

Ultron builds the trigger to his doomsday device in a ruined church at the exact center of Sokovia's capital. This ancient building becomes the focus of the battle, as the Avengers try desperately (and unsuccessfully) to prevent the weapon being activated.

Though the Avengers succeed in thwarting Ultron's plans, they have to destroy Sokovia in the process. Thousands of civilians are evacuated, but hundreds die. The destruction of Sokovia ultimately leads to the Sokovia Accords which, in turn, cause the Avengers Civil War.

Links to vast machinery buried beneath

Activation will cause Sokovia to fall to Earth

Pedestal originally held throne

Pincers hold detonator in place

Vision—the newest Avenger—takes no pleasure in destroying Ultron's last sentry, effectively killing him. Ultron may be evil, but in some ways he is also Vision's closest kin.

VISION

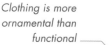
Head covering focuses consciousness

Mind Stone mounted in forehead

Vision is a synthezoid—a self-aware, synthetic being who is neither human nor machine. Although his body was created by Ultron, in outlook the two of them could not be more different. Vision is a benevolent being who can fly, become incorporeal, and shoot energy beams from his forehead. At first, the Avengers are unsure of Vision's intentions, but when he lifts Thor's hammer, Mjolnir, the synthezoid proves his purity and worthiness to become an Avenger. He joins them in their final defeat of Ultron.

Clothing is more ornamental than functional

Ultron designed a physically perfect body

Ultron's forefather is JARVIS, Tony Stark's artificial intelligence system, responsible for assisting him with his business and Super Hero activities. Tony shows Bruce Banner a golden holographic representation of JARVIS during their experiments to create the new Ultron A.I.

BORN YESTERDAY

Ultron creates what will later become Vision's body by combining vibranium metal with artificial human cells and adding an Infinity Stone. Ultron is interrupted before he can download his own consciousness into the body, however, and Tony Stark downloads JARVIS into the body instead.

Auto-lock lid

Diagnostic screen displays vital signs

Control panel

REGENERATION CRADLE

Dr. Cho's Regeneration Cradle is intended to help patients heal wounds by printing synthetic tissue onto the affected site, then tricking the body's own cells into binding with it. In the case of Vision, it creates an entire new body.

Ultron forces Dr. Cho to build a new body for him—though the Avengers then steal it.

DR. CHO

Helen Cho is a top geneticist who aids the Avengers when Hawkeye is gravely wounded. Her cutting-edge breakthroughs in body tissue regeneration help him recover, but also make her useful to Ultron's plans for a body upgrade.

Cape is inspired by Thor's own

Thor has a vision warning him of a coming threat—and that this new synthezoid will play a key role in fighting it. Just when the other Avengers want to prevent the body from awakening, fearing another Ultron, Thor arrives and provides the necessary jolt of lightning to bring his "Vision" to life.

Vision emulates the other Avengers by manifesting a costume for himself, complete with gauntlets

DATA FILE

> The gem mounted in Loki's scepter is the Mind Stone—one of six Infinity Stones. It bestows Vision with consciousness, but Vision's roots as JARVIS are clear—he retains the clipped British accent of Stark's A.I. assistant.

> During the Battle of Sokovia, Vision prevents Ultron from escaping by blocking his access to the internet. This allows the Avengers to hunt down and destroy Ultron's individual bodies.

Vision emerges from the Regeneration Cradle fully formed and mature. He is highly intelligent, fully aware, and knowledgeable of the circumstances of his creation. At first he lunges at Thor, but after a brief moment is calm and apologizes to him.

Vision approaches dilemmas like the Sokovia Accords with patience and consideration. He isn't prone to emotional appeals and doesn't respond in anger.

Infinity Stone

NAVIGATING HUMANITY

Vision knows he is neither like Ultron nor like humans. He is something different, in-between, unencumbered by self-serving ambition or self-destructive ego. He values the fragility of human life and its endeavors to become something better. Vision is drawn to Wanda Maximoff, though he is shy about expressing his feelings. He feels a bond with her, in part because the Infinity Stone that gave him life also gave Wanda her powers. He struggles to understand boundaries of personal space and privacy, though, even entering rooms through the walls which can irritate Wanda.

INFINITE POWER
One of Vision's most powerful weapons is the ability to shoot a beam of unknown energy from the Infinity Stone in his forehead.

THANOS

Known as the "Mad Titan" by the galactic community, villainous Thanos is by far the greatest threat that the Avengers and their allies have ever faced. Thanos is a being of almost limitless power, relentlessly driven by his goal to seize the six Infinity Stones from their various keepers. His monstrous plan is to combine their powers and arbitrarily wipe out half of the beings in the universe—a catastrophic feat that he will be able to carry out with just a snap of his fingers.

Golden chestplate with high collar lends powerful air

Shrewd smirk shows cunning personality

Broad, sloping shoulders

Purple skin due to genetic deformity

Infinity Gauntlet curled into fist of triumph

Geometric design common in Titan culture

Thickly muscled limbs

Heavy boots have stomped the surfaces of many worlds

After witnessing the environmental destruction wrought by overpopulation on his homeworld, Thanos resolves to spare the rest of the universe the same fate by massacring half of the population of every planet. Thanos knows the universe has finite resources, and believes he is the only one willing to take on the responsibility of culling life to redress the balance.

Thanos spared Gamora from massacre as a child and adopted her, trying to teach her the necessity of his vision. Thanos' boundless cruelty belies the fact that he bears a deep love for Gamora.

MASTER MANIPULATOR

Thanos is effectively invincible—he can hold the Infinity Stones in his bare hands without being destroyed, an act very few in the universe are capable of. He is also ruthlessly calculating, and highly skilled at bending even the most powerful beings to his will. But Thanos is not without mercy; in his own twisted way, he believes that his actions are both a kindness and a small price to pay, so that those left alive may avoid future conflict and starvation.

DATA FILE

> Doctor Strange searches the future to learn possible outcomes of the battle with Thanos. There are more than 14 million futures where Thanos wins, and only one where he loses.

> A fake version of the Infinity Gauntlet was found in Odin's vault on Asgard, prior to Asgard's destruction. Unlike the real one, the fake version was right-handed.

INFINITY STONES

The Infinity Stones are the condensed remains of six singularities that existed long before the current universe. Every stone holds a power so vast that it lies beyond mortal comprehension. Each controls a primordial aspect of the universe: space, reality, time, power, mind, and soul. To wield all six stones at once, Thanos forces the master craftsman Eitri of Nidavellir to forge a mighty weapon to hold them: the Infinity Gauntlet. As Thanos takes the stones one by one from his foes, he places them into the Gauntlet, like a jeweled trophy.

SPACE STONE
Once contained in the Tesseract, the Space Stone can facilitate interdimensional travel, or act as a source of arcane energy.

REALITY STONE
Also known as the Aether, the Reality Stone can alter the fabric of reality and convert matter to dark matter.

TIME STONE
Formerly set in the Eye of Agamotto, this stone can manipulate the passage of time, changing past or future.

POWER STONE
Previously held in the vaults of Xandar, the Power Stone emits energy that can destroy almost any known object or substance.

MIND STONE
This stone once formed part of the synthezoid Vision. It can control minds, and bestow beings with super-powers.

SOUL STONE
Guarded by Red Skull on the planet Vormir, Thanos must sacrifice a loved one's soul in exchange for the stone. Its powers are still to be revealed.

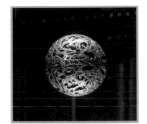

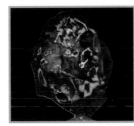

Reality Stone

Soul Stone

Space Stone

Power Stone

Mind Stone

Time Stone

Uru metal forged in furnaces powered by dying star

Segmented Dwarven-style decoration

Gauntlet designed to fit tightly over Thanos' left forearm

INFINITY GAUNTLET

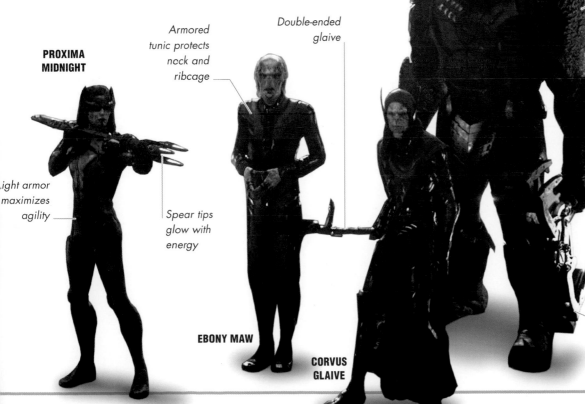

CULL OBSIDIAN

Thick reptilian skin absorbs attacks

PROXIMA MIDNIGHT

Armored tunic protects neck and ribcage

Double-ended glaive

Light armor maximizes agility

Spear tips glow with energy

EBONY MAW

CORVUS GLAIVE

CHILDREN OF THANOS

Thanos is aided in his quest by several of his adopted children—individuals he deemed worth sparing when he attacked their homeworlds. Each has unique skills and abilities that make them fearsome warriors: Ebony Maw's powers of telekinesis are immense, Corvus Glaive and Proxima Midnight are master combatants with their chosen weapons, and Cull Obsidian possesses tremendous strength and durability. Unlike Thanos' rogue daughters Gamora and Nebula, these four remain his loyal servants and obey Thanos' every command.

Hammer has multiple functions: melee weapon, claw, shield, and projectile weapon

INFINITY WAR

||||||||||||||||||||||||||||||||||||

Across the cosmos, the final stages of Thanos' plan are in motion. Everything has been leading to this moment: the Infinity Stones are almost within his grasp, and the universe stares into the abyss. Earth holds two of the Infinity Stones, and Thanos' eye turns once more to this small, blue planet. Earth's greatest defenders, the Avengers, are divided and vulnerable. The heaviest of blows is about to be struck, and defeat looks inevitable.

Following the break-up of the Avengers, a blossoming romance has developed between Scarlet Witch and Vision. They have also gained greater mastery over their respective powers, and Wanda is now capable of destroying an Infinity Stone. Vision's Mind Stone makes him one of two main targets on Earth, and two of Thanos' children viciously attack the pair in Scotland.

Cybernetic eye given to him by Rocket

Muscles mistaken for Cotati metal fibers

A DESPERATE GOD

Following Thanos' attack on Thor's spaceship, the *Ark*, Thor has lost everything. This vengeful god joins forces with the Guardians of the Galaxy and is determined to defeat Thanos at any cost.

Loki saved the Tesseract from Asgard's vault and secretly kept it on board the *Ark*. When Thanos attacks the ship, Loki attempts to do the right thing by tricking the Titan in an attempt to kill him. Thanos sees through Loki's lies and kills the god of mischief.

Royal disks can conduct electricity

Somber colors reflect Thor's mournful nature

THOR

CAPTAIN AMERICA

Neck protection

Plain pauldrons

Accumulated battle damage

Blond hair less recognizable than her traditional color

BLACK WIDOW

Bulletproof jacket

AVENGERS REASSEMBLED

When Vision and Scarlet Witch are attacked in Scotland by Corvus Glaive and Proxima Midnight, Cap and his team rush to their aid. This sets them on a path that forces them out of the shadows to protect the Earth from Thanos.

Ever since the Avengers split apart, Captain America, Falcon, and Black Widow have been on the run from the authorities. They travel the world in an unmarked Quinjet, fighting evil wherever they can.

Subdued colors to avoid detection

DATA FILE

> An advanced powered exo-skeleton allows Colonel Rhodes (a.k.a. War Machine) to walk despite his paralysis.

> After the Avengers' Civil War, both Hawkeye and Ant-Man are under house arrest, spending time with their families.

Staff can detach into two batons

Sleeves rolled up ready for action

Nanobot surface can regenerate following battle damage

Silver highlights added to iconic red-and-gold armor color scheme

Repulsor beams can easily cut through alien materials

MARK 50

After 49 previous suits of armor, Iron Man's Mark 50 is an extremely advanced piece of technology. It is stored as nano-tech within Tony's latest Arc Reactor/Repulsor Tech node (RT) and can seamlessly adapt to Iron Man's needs in battle. For a time, Tony can even hold his own against Thanos, with the suit reforming itself into many powerful weapons.

Once again, New York City suffers at the hands of Thanos. Warned by Bruce Banner's sudden arrival, Tony Stark, Doctor Strange, and Wong must join forces with him to protect the Time Stone, held in Strange's Eye of Agamotto, from Ebony Maw and Cull Obsidian.

After Peter Parker assisted him in the battle against Steve Rogers' group of Avengers, Tony Stark created a new, high-tech suit—code-named Item 17A—for Spider-Man. Parker dons this intuitive suit, which has four additional, retractable legs and powerful web shooters, during the journey to Titan.

Suit's thrusters are faster than previous models

Much like other teenagers, Groot enjoys video games

TEENAGE GROOT

Time has passed since the Guardians' battle with Ego, and Baby Groot has entered his teenage years. Groot is sullen and shows little interest in unfolding events, but he is willing to lend a branch at critical moments to protect or to help his friends.

Tony Stark used to have nightmares about finding himself on the other side of the galaxy. Now the nightmare is real. After crash-landing on Titan—Thanos' desolate homeworld—Stark, Doctor Strange, and Spider-Man bump into the Guardians. They must all work together on a plan to defeat Thanos.

New vines indicate imminent growth spurt

BATTLE OF WAKANDA

The plains surrounding Wakanda's capital, Birnin Zana, become the final battleground on Earth against Thanos. The Avengers and their allies must desperately hold back his army, while Shuri attempts to detach the Mind Stone from Vision's forehead so it can be destroyed. Birnin Zana's protective energy shield and the Wakandans' advanced weaponry make this a very different conflict to the first Battle of New York years before, but the arrival of Thanos tips the odds against the Avengers.

Unleashed from their dropships, Thanos' vicious army of Outriders swarms across the lush plains of Wakanda. The horde appears infinite, and Falcon's airborne assault seems to make little dent to their numbers.

ANT-MAN

Take an ex-convict with a heart of gold, ally him with a genius Cold War secret agent and his no-nonsense daughter, give him a mission to save the world, and you have a recipe for a Super Hero unlike any other. What would it be like to be the size of an insect, but still have the strength of a full-grown human? What if you could control ants, giving you a vast army of tiny warriors? What if you had the power to shrink or grow anything around you at will? Ant-Man can do all of these things, and much more.

"WHY DON'T YOU PICK ON SOMEONE YOUR OWN SIZE?"

SCOTT LANG

ANT-MAN

Scott Lang is an ex-criminal and ally of the Avengers. He has a good heart and means well, but his desperation to be united with his daughter coupled with poor judgment motivates him to rush into precarious situations. He meets the former Ant-Man, Hank Pym and Hank's daughter, Hope Van Dyne, after robbing their residence—in reality a trap set by Pym to recruit Lang as his successor. Pym equips Lang with an Ant-Man suit that allows him to shrink and grow at will, and the ability to communicate with ants.

Scott Lang's daughter Cassie believes in him, despite his criminal activities. His lifestyle threatens his visitation rights though. Lang's desire to be a part of her life again motivates him to become a better man.

Multi-hinged shoulder armor

Stretchable red armor plating

Restore-size button

Helmet mandible locking joint

CRIMINAL TALENT

Lang's crimes weren't purely for self-gain. He spent three years in San Quentin State Prison for robbing his former employer, but this was after he discovered they were overcharging customers. Hank Pym believes Lang's skills as a thief and desire to help others make him the perfect candidate to take over as Ant-Man. Ironically, his first mission is a heist: He must steal weaponized Pym technology from Hank's evil protégé, Darren Cross, before it falls into the wrong hands.

Scott has a Masters in electrical engineering. This background equips him with many skills necessary for complex robberies. He uses liquid nitrogen and water to expand the door of Hank Pym's safe and break it open. Finding only the Ant-Man suit, Lang steals it, unknowingly falling into Pym's trap.

Confused face, owing to discovery that Pym's safe is (almost) empty

Communications antennae

Black pearlized leather

Pheromone anklets keep ants docile

Elbowed antennae with
right-angle bend

Large wings make
carpenter ants
adept fliers

Saddle with handlebars

ANT-THONY

Hank Pym has so many ants that he gives them
numbers rather than names. The one that Lang calls
"Ant-Thony" is Number 247. Lang develops a close
bond with Ant-Thony after the winged carpenter ant
helps him escape from police custody and flies him
on several missions. Ant-Thony is friendly and a loyal
steed. Sadly, he is shot down by Darren Cross.

Scott Lang's use of the Ant-Man
suit puts him in great danger. Its
powers give him an advantage, but
insignificant things can suddenly
become mountainous obstacles.
Though some adversaries are
perilous at any size, Yellowjacket
(Darren Cross) is the only one who
can battle Ant-Man at his own scale.

Scott Lang's training requires him to not only get accustomed to working directly with
swarms of ants on their level, but also developing personal relationships with some
of them. This marks a big transition, as Scott is initially terrified of the insects.

GIANT-MAN

Pym Particles are the key to Ant-Man's technology.
Discovered by Hank Pym, they can alter the size of
any object. Lang later develops a new application
of Pym Particles that allows him grow to a giant
size. He has only tried it once prior to unveiling it
in the battle at Leipzig-Halle, and worries about
passing out—or even being ripped in half!

Refined particle tubing
allows Lang to become
"Giant Man" without
gruesome side effects

Indicator lights change
color depending on
Pym Particles: red for
shrinking and blue
for expansion

New suit has more
streamlined helmet

Upgraded fabric is
more flexible than
the original

While battling Iron Man at Leipzig-Halle
Airport, Lang shrinks and slips inside Iron
Man's armor to dismantle it from the
inside. Lang finds the Mark XLVI
suit's interior rather roomy as he
unplugs electrical wires. Stark
is forced to turn on his armor's
internal fire suppression system
to flush Lang out.

ANT-MAN TECH

||||||||||||||||||||||||||||||||||||||||||||||||||||||||

Ant-Man's technology is based on two principles. The first is his ability to change size by using Pym Particles, named after their discoverer, Hank Pym. All matter is largely made up of the empty space between atoms. Pym Particles reduce that space, thus compressing matter and shrinking a person or object. Ant-Man uses a suit to regulate his intake of particles. In addition to the stealth benefits of being small, he can concentrate his strength in powerful bursts. His second tech-based advantage comes from his ability to influence ants to aid him in many innovative ways.

Visor swings up to open

Formic acid shield and anti-glare visor

Speaker and air filter

HELMET
The Ant-Man helmet protects the brain from dangerous chemical imbalances caused by Pym Particles. A button on the right-hand side parts the mandibles and swings the face plate up to reveal Scott Lang's face.

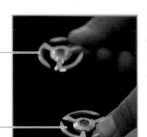

Blue enlarges target

Red shrinks target

PYM PARTICLE DISKS
Ant-Man carries Pym Particle Disks on his belt. These can be thrown at something to change its size by releasing Pym Particles on contact.

Pym Particle circulation tubing

Vials of Pym Particles

ANT-MAN SUIT

The Ant-Man suit was created by Hank Pym for his covert missions with S.H.I.E.L.D. The suit regulates the flow of Pym Particles, allowing the wearer to easily control their size. It has armor plating for intense physical combat and can support other gadgets like flamethrowers and grappling guns. Hank Pym tells Scott Lang that the Iron Man suit is "cute" in comparison.

EMP COMMUNICATION DEVICE
Hank Pym teaches Lang to use an earpiece that reads his brainwaves and translates them into electromagnetic waves. The waves then stimulate ants' olfactory nerves, sending them commands. Scott tests it by making them deliver sugar cubes.

Tubes dispense Pym Particles

SUIT CONTROLS
There is a button on each glove controlled by the thumb. The right glove button shrinks Ant-Man, the left restores him to normal size. A touch-screen on the right gauntlet of Lang's upgraded suit allows him to recalibrate his size changes. His belt contains a regulator and supply of Pym Particles.

Gloves comprised of 46 different components

GAUNTLETS

Regulator

Pym Particle holder

UTILITY BELT

ANT SPECIES

Ant-Man spends a lot of time the size of an insect, so it helps to have insect-sized allies. Ants are useful partners because they can lift 50 times their own weight and they cooperate naturally. In addition, they are everywhere; they are native to every continent except Antarctica and are believed to comprise the largest percentage of the world's terrestrial animal biomass (up to 25 percent). There are more than 12,500 known species of ant worldwide—many with special skills.

Monodomous (single-nest) colony

Polydomous (multi-nest) colony

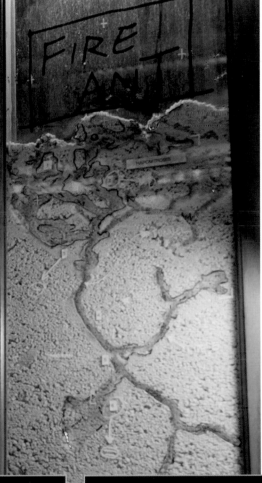

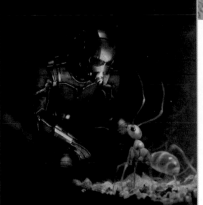

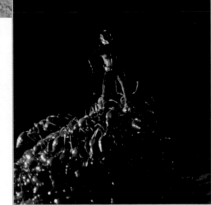

CARPENTER ANTS

Camponotus pennsylvanicus, or black carpenter ants, are a large species that live in colonies in decaying wood. They are strong and have a powerful bite, but their most useful ability is flight, and Ant-Man uses them for transportation.

BULLET ANTS

Paraponera clavata, commonly known as bullet ants, are famous for their powerful sting. They are rated highest for pain ("Level 4") on the Schmidt Sting Pain Index. Bullet ants are native to lowland rainforests in Nicaragua, Paraguay, and Honduras.

CRAZY ANTS

Nylanderia fulva are known as raspberry crazy ants, or just crazy ants. These South American ants have a habit of running around erratically and forming gargantuan swarms in an instant. They are good at carrying equipment and can conduct electricity.

FIRE ANTS

Solenopsis mandibularis or fire ants are found from the Southeastern United States southward to Venezuela and Columbia. Though they are potent stingers, their most useful ability is the forming of makeshift structures like bridges and rafts.

HOPE VAN DYNE

Chairwoman of the board at Pym Technologies, bristly Hope Van Dyne is blunt and abrupt by nature. Daughter of Janet Van Dyne and Hank Pym, Hope is fiercely intelligent, a martial arts maestro, and an expert in her father's Ant-Man technology. Hope's relationship with Hank grew strained following her mother's supposed death, leaving Hope embittered. The two reconcile after they recruit Scott Lang to sabotage a villain's plans to sell Pym technology to terrorists. Hope goes on to wear her mother's Wasp suit and become a size-shifting Super Hero alongside Ant-Man.

Chin-length, glossy bob

Her mother Janet's necklace

Smart business attire has clean, tailored lines

PAST REGRETS

Hope cast the deciding vote to oust her father from his own company when Hank's protégé, Darren Cross, turned against Hank and tried to convince the board to remove him. She regretted that decision once Cross became CEO. Growing evermore suspicious of Cross' motives, she spies on him for her father, in the hope they can regain control of the company.

Hope watches with horror as Darren Cross militarizes her father's technology. She'd like to intervene, but doesn't have that authority. Instead she monitors the progress of his research so she and her father will know how much time they have to stop him.

Everlast C3 Evercool professional headgear

Martial arts training gloves

Hesitant stance of a novice

Hope is good with insects. She teaches Scott about the four species of ants they use: bullet, fire, crazy, and carpenter—before he shrinks down and encounters them at their own size.

TRAINING SCOTT

Hope trains Lang to use the Ant-Man suit's abilities to his advantage. Exploiting these abilities is tricky, though. It is hard to gauge how much force to use. Too much and Scott could easily kill someone—Hope says his strikes would be equivalent to a bullet. Scott overstates his prison fighting experience, so Hope must also teach him how to throw a punch.

Pointed high heels

HER MOTHER'S LEGACY

Janet Van Dyne served in S.H.I.E.L.D. alongside Pym. Taking the codename Wasp, she joined him on operations as a fellow ant-sized warrior. She disappeared on a mission, heroically shrinking down to the Quantum Realm to slip inside the shell of a rogue nuclear missile aimed at the United States. Hope wants to carry on her mother's legacy more than anything. She is more agile, more skilled at using the Ant-Man suit, and better at working with ants than Scott Lang or even her own father.

Hope's inside knowledge of Darren Cross' project is vital for planning their heist at Pym Tech. Hope thinks she should be the one in the Ant-Man suit (and rightly so), but Hank insists they need her close enough to spy on Cross instead.

Grappling line ties
Janet to missile

DATA FILE

> Hope trains Lang in her father's basement. To begin with, she thinks Lang is an incompetent idiot.

> Hope calls her father "Hank" to upset him, but reverts to calling him "Dad" after Cross shoots him.

The Quantum Realm, where Janet was lost, is a dimension where size regresses infinitely and time has no meaning. It lies beyond molecules, atoms, and even the fundamental building blocks of matter: protons, neutrons, and electrons.

Helmet
protects brain
chemistry

Protective lens

High-performance
insect-like wings

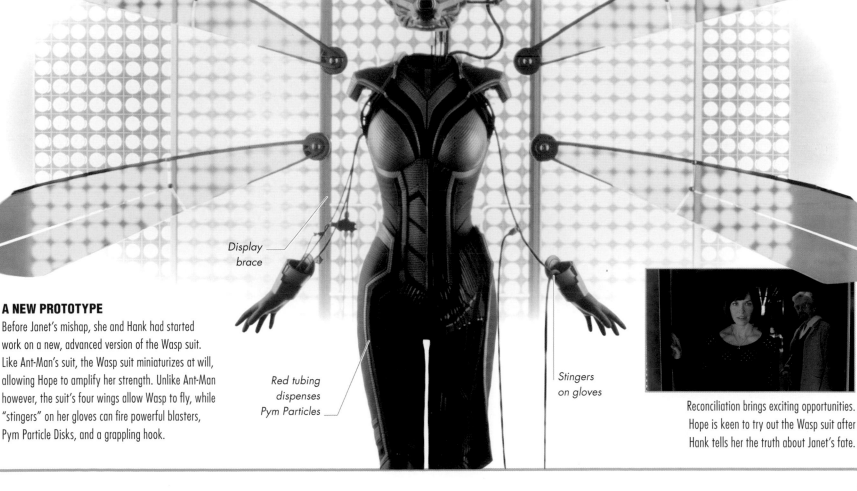

Display
brace

A NEW PROTOTYPE

Before Janet's mishap, she and Hank had started work on a new, advanced version of the Wasp suit. Like Ant-Man's suit, the Wasp suit miniaturizes at will, allowing Hope to amplify her strength. Unlike Ant-Man however, the suit's four wings allow Wasp to fly, while "stingers" on her gloves can fire powerful blasters, Pym Particle Disks, and a grappling hook.

Red tubing
dispenses
Pym Particles

Stingers
on gloves

Reconciliation brings exciting opportunities. Hope is keen to try out the Wasp suit after Hank tells her the truth about Janet's fate.

HANK PYM

Dr. Henry "Hank" Pym is the original Ant-Man and the discoverer of Pym Particles. He is a scientist with a secret history full of action, adventure, and espionage, who hides his past behind a stern, no-nonsense persona. Pym is devoted to his daughter, Hope, but his over-protectiveness causes resentment in her that drives them apart. Eventually, Pym is pushed out of his own company, Pym Technology, and now desperately seeks a new apprentice to help him keep his Ant-Man technology from falling into the wrong hands.

Pym's wife, Janet Van Dyne (code name: Wasp), joined him on operations, wearing her own size-changing suit. During a 1987 mission to stop a rogue Soviet missile, Janet shrank too far and was lost to the Quantum Realm.

Pair of Old Focals' clear Advocate glasses

Single-breasted three-piece suit with notched lapel

FIRST ANT-MAN

Dr. Pym is a retired physicist and entomologist. He worked for S.H.I.E.L.D. as a consultant and agent, using his Ant-Man suit to go on missions during the Cold War. Pym resigned in 1989 after discovering Mitchell Carson (a Hydra double agent) was leading attempts to duplicate his Ant-Man technology behind his back— all with Howard Stark's approval. Decades later, Pym tells Lang "You never can trust a Stark."

After leaving S.H.I.E.L.D., Pym founds Pym Technologies as a way to finance his search for his missing wife. The company specializes in nanotechnology and atomic research.

Hank Pym lives in an old Victorian manor built in the late 1800s. The cozy San Francisco home is full of antique furniture and curiosities, hinting at his adventures as Ant-Man.

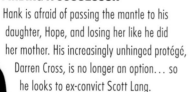

FINDING A SUCCESSOR

Hank is afraid of passing the mantle to his daughter, Hope, and losing her like he did her mother. His increasingly unhinged protégé, Darren Cross, is no longer an option... so he looks to ex-convict Scott Lang.

DATA FILE

> Pym's tank-shaped key chain is actually a shrunk T-34 Soviet battle tank. Hank knows having an instant tank might come in handy.

> When Lang suggests they call the Avengers, Pym retorts "they're probably too busy dropping cities out of the sky," referring to Sokovia.

ANT-MAN'S ALLIES

Scott Lang's heroics as Ant-Man wouldn't be possible without a diverse group of allies. Lang's fellow ex-convicts Luis, Dave, and Kurt, each play vital roles in helping him break into Pym Tech, while Detective Jim Paxton is an unlikely enemy-turned-ally. Paxton got engaged to Lang's ex-wife Maggie while Lang was in prison; he, Maggie, and Lang's daughter, Cassie, live together at 840 Winter Street in San Francisco. Although he is initially suspicious of Lang, Paxton helps clear the criminal charges against him after Lang rescues Cassie from Darren Cross.

JIM PAXTON

Detective Jim Paxton is devoted to Maggie and her daughter Cassie, but disapproves of Lang's criminal past. He spends most of his time either steering Lang away, or trying to arrest him. Scott's bravery in rescuing Cassie changes Paxton's mind about him.

LUIS

Luis is Scott Lang's best friend and former prison cellmate. After Lang is released from San Quentin State Prison, he moves in with Luis at the Milgrom Hotel in San Francisco. He is a cheerful and funny guy, even in adversity, but struggles to stay focused.

KURT

Kurt is an Eastern European computer hacker who spent five years in Folsom State Prison. He specializes in disabling security systems, helping Lang break into Hank Pym's house, and then later, Pym Tech.

DAVE

Dave is the team's gruff getaway driver. He's the most standoffish of the three, taking longer to warm up to Lang. Hank Pym calls Dave, Luis, and Kurt "those three wombats" due to their odd personalities.

Beanie rolled up so it does not obstruct Dave's view on the job

Cups of strong coffee keep Dave alert for quick getaways

Carefully groomed sideburns

YELLOWJACKET

Darren Cross is an MIT valedictorian and former protégé of Hank Pym. Driven by ambition, paranoia, and the desire to surpass his old boss, Cross, now CEO of Pym Tech, attempts to recreate Pym's Ant-Man research and develop his own size-changing suit. He attempts to sell this militarized "Yellowjacket" technology to assorted terrorist groups, but is thwarted by Hank Pym, Hope Van Dyne, and Scott Lang, who destroy Cross' research and put an end to the villain once and for all.

Cross invites Hank Pym and Hope Van Dyne to an event at Pym Technologies. There, he shows a video exposing Hank Pym's secret-agent past and announces the company is developing products based on the Ant-Man.

ARMORED VILLAIN

The Yellowjacket suit is an armored size-changing outfit much like Ant-Man's, but weaponized for warfare. Unlike Ant-Man, Yellowjacket can fly, thanks to booster rockets in the back. His retractable arms can be used for climbing and manipulating objects, too. They are tipped with "stingers" that fire lasers capable of incinerating hardened targets.

Retractable antenna housing

Colorful, sleek design intended to upstage Pym's old-fashioned Ant-Man suit

Charge cell for laser cannon

Military-grade Kevlar fabric

Legs retract onto backpack

Belt pumps circulate Pym Particles

Sensor and communications antennae

Molecular respirator

Titanium helmet

Retractable faceplate

Backpack harness

Joint servos

Control bracelet

Reinforced combat gauntlets

Powerful titanium limbs

High-powered laser

Experimental coating intended to reflect energy weapons

Fabric instead of metal plates allows great freedom of movement, crucial for hand-to-hand combat

Extra plates shield vulnerable joints

Yellowjacket can change size at will, much like Ant-Man. His suit uses an array of systems to regulate size, though these prototype systems are imperfect, and Yellowjacket's main danger is shrinking unevenly, which could cause him to implode.

STUDENT BECOMES MASTER

Cross was like a son to Pym, but his ambition and suspicious obsession with Pym's research drove a wedge between them. After he had Pym kicked out of his own company, Cross was promoted to CEO.

Impact-absorbing soles

Stretchable fabric

Fire-resistant boots

Darren Cross' ruthlessness is demonstrated when he uses Scott Lang's daughter, Cassie, as bait to lure Lang for a final confrontation. The two switch back and forth between sizes, turning Cassie's bedroom full of toys into a deadly battle zone.

Straps distribute weight of backpack

Cross has a difficult time duplicating Hank Pym's results with Pym Particles. His initial trials using lambs are failures, resulting in puddles of protein goo. Cross also isn't aware of the changes in brain chemistry caused by Pym Particles. His failure to adequately shield his brain exacerbates his own mental instability.

lamb successfully miniaturized

DATA FILE

> Cross is in the process of rebranding Pym Technologies as Cross Technologies when he meets his demise at the hands of Scott Lang.

> Before he is able to shrink living things safely, Darren Cross adapts his unstable Pym Particles for use as a weapon. His prototype shrink-gun reduces people to tiny pieces of proteinaceous slime.

BLACK PANTHER

Millions of years ago, a meteorite struck the center of Africa. This was no ordinary meteorite, however. It was made from vibranium, the strongest substance in the universe. When humanity arose to claim the world, five tribes settled on the site of the meteorite. They called their realm Wakanda, and they learned to exploit the vibranium and the mutated plant life that it caused. They used its powers to create a guardian—a mighty warrior sworn to protect Wakanda. Over the centuries there would be many such guardians, but all would share the same title: the Black Panther.

"IF ANYONE FOUND OUT WHAT WE TRULY ARE, WHAT WE POSSESS... IT COULD DESTROY THE WORLD."

T'CHALLA

BLACK PANTHER

Prince T'Challa holds the ancient title of Black Panther—the sworn protector of Wakanda. He wears a protective vibranium suit with deadly claws, and his super-speed, strength, and resilience come from a rare heart-shaped herb. T'Challa becomes king of Wakanda when his father is killed in a terrorist bombing. After taking the throne, T'Challa transforms his secretive country into a model and protector for the world. The kind-hearted T'Challa proves it is indeed possible for a good man to be a king.

T'Challa loves and respects his father T'Chaka, and is with him at the signing of the Sokovia Accords when T'Chaka is killed by a bomb, supposedly planted by the Winter Soldier. Frustrated by his inability to save his father, T'Challa yearns for retribution.

Suit's solid mask is removed manually

Ear microphones with adjustable sensitivity

Abrasive palms for better grip

Retractable vibranium claws

Reinforced vibranium frame for added strength

T'Challa's desire to kill the Winter Soldier in order to avenge his father puts him in direct conflict with Steve Rogers.

Reinforced shoulder armor

Eye shields in closed position

Stylized vibranium panther claws

The Black Panther sides with Iron Man in the Avengers' internal conflict. He doesn't share Tony Stark's concern about apprehending former team members. T'Challa only wants vengeance.

Chest plates contain vital-signs sensors

DEFENDER OF WAKANDA

Naturally, the first priority of the prince and future king of Wakanda is the wellbeing of his country. Wakanda has always kept its technological advances a secret to protect itself. Likewise, when he is overseas, T'Challa hides his connection to the Black Panther. He uses the Black Panther suit only when he must protect his family and people. Like all of T'Challa's equipment, this flexible yet almost indestructible combat armor was built for him by his brilliant engineer sister, Shuri.

Vibranium threads woven into fabric

ORIGINAL SUIT

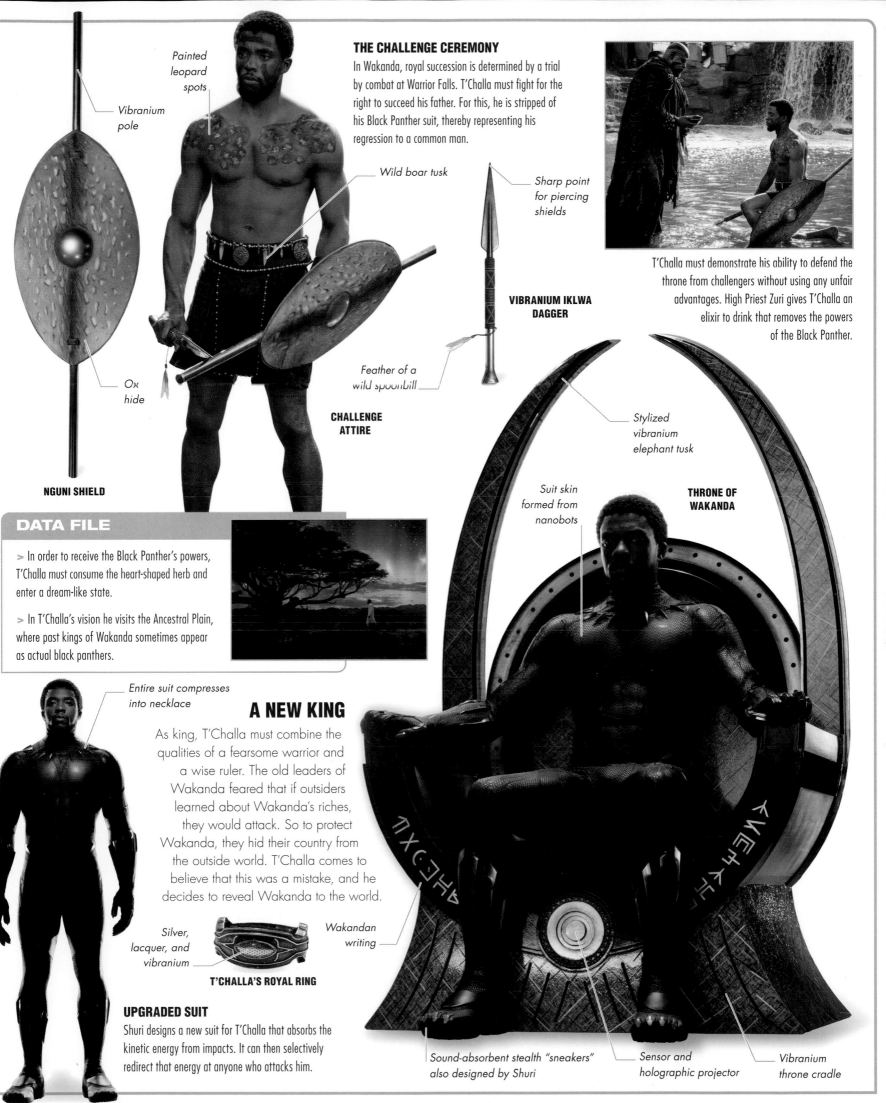

Vibranium pole

Painted leopard spots

Vibranium pole

Wild boar tusk

THE CHALLENGE CEREMONY

In Wakanda, royal succession is determined by a trial by combat at Warrior Falls. T'Challa must fight for the right to succeed his father. For this, he is stripped of his Black Panther suit, thereby representing his regression to a common man.

Sharp point for piercing shields

VIBRANIUM IKLWA DAGGER

T'Challa must demonstrate his ability to defend the throne from challengers without using any unfair advantages. High Priest Zuri gives T'Challa an elixir to drink that removes the powers of the Black Panther.

Ox hide

Feather of a wild spoonbill

NGUNI SHIELD

CHALLENGE ATTIRE

Stylized vibranium elephant tusk

Suit skin formed from nanobots

THRONE OF WAKANDA

DATA FILE

> In order to receive the Black Panther's powers, T'Challa must consume the heart-shaped herb and enter a dream-like state.

> In T'Challa's vision he visits the Ancestral Plain, where past kings of Wakanda sometimes appear as actual black panthers.

Entire suit compresses into necklace

A NEW KING

As king, T'Challa must combine the qualities of a fearsome warrior and a wise ruler. The old leaders of Wakanda feared that if outsiders learned about Wakanda's riches, they would attack. So to protect Wakanda, they hid their country from the outside world. T'Challa comes to believe that this was a mistake, and he decides to reveal Wakanda to the world.

Silver, lacquer, and vibranium

Wakandan writing

T'CHALLA'S ROYAL RING

UPGRADED SUIT

Shuri designs a new suit for T'Challa that absorbs the kinetic energy from impacts. It can then selectively redirect that energy at anyone who attacks him.

Sound-absorbent stealth "sneakers" also designed by Shuri

Sensor and holographic projector

Vibranium throne cradle

143

PEOPLE OF WAKANDA

Wakanda is a small country located in Central Africa. It is the most technologically advanced nation on Earth, but hides its wealth and resources under the guise of a developing country. Its people have a rich culture and are highly educated; they speak the African language Xhosa and have a unique written alphabet. There are five tribes, and the Wakandan monarch is answerable to a council of their tribal elders.

M'BAKU'S MASK

M'BAKU

A towering powerhouse of a man, M'Baku is the leader of the vegetarian Jabari Tribe. His people live high in the snowy peaks of Wakanda, away from the rest of society. They shun the use of vibranium technology, yet M'Baku has still accumulated great wealth, symbolized by the strings of cowrie shells that he often wears.

M'Baku's mountaintop palace is a blend of traditional styles and modern innovations. Its smooth hardwood floors lead toward an austere throne perched above breathtaking views. The Jabari use wood instead of vibranium, and over millennia have become masterful carpenters.

W'KABI

Until he betrays Prince T'Challa, W'Kabi is his closest friend. W'Kabi is the leader of the Border Tribe and Okoye's husband. IIe lives in the fertile Wakandan highlands, where he raises rhinos.

Fur represents silverback gorilla

Ebony pauldron protects shoulders

Knobkerrie (club-staff weapon)

Hand-carved chest armor

Fur arm-wraps for cold mountain weather

Studded gauntlets

Whittled wooden shaft

Grass skirt for warmth

Kneecap protector

Studs for offensive kicks

Hand-sewn leather shoes

Very ancient ceremonial spearhead

Symbol of priesthood

ZURI

Zuri is the king's closest advisor and high priest of Wakanda. He is a kind-hearted man, yet haunted by the regret of abandoning Erik Killmonger as a child. Zuri serves both T'Chaka and T'Challa, until he is murdered by Killmonger (who knew Zuri as his "Uncle James").

Zuri officiates the Challenge Ceremony and coronation of T'Challa. It is his honor to bestow and rescind the powers of the Black Panther.

Agbada-style ceremonial robe

Tabard decorated with bones, wood, and beads

SPEAR OF BASHENGA

3D-printed headdress echoes Zulu fashions

Obsidian earrings

Natural sapphire

RAMONDA

Queen Ramonda is the widow of King T'Chaka and mother to T'Challa and Shuri. She is devoted to her family and the wellbeing of her country. Her love, courage, and strength inspires her children to fight back against the usurper Killmonger.

Kimoyo music bead

After T'Challa becomes king, Ramonda continues to sit on the council of elders that advise him in the royal throne room.

Train holds dirt-repelling fibers

Earthquake-proof architecture

Public library

University tower

Outdoor shopping plaza

Community hospital

BIRNIN ZANA

Wakanda's capital city, Birnin Zana, lies hidden beneath a holographic projection of forested hills that also blocks foreign radar and satellites. Protected from direct attack by an energy shield, the futuristic city of skyscrapers and high-speed trams straddles a river that runs through an otherwise pristine valley. The bustling municipality is the center of government, education, art, and shopping. Downtown markets erupt with colorful fashions and tantalizing aromas of African fusion cuisine.

DATA FILE

> The totem of M'Baku's Jabari Tribe is the White Ape rather than Black Panther. They are also devotees of the monkey god Hanuman.

> Wakanda was founded by the warrior Bashenga, who became the first Black Panther after he discovered the heart-shaped herb.

NAKIA

Nakia is a high-ranking member of Wakanda's River Tribe, a first class spy, a fearless warrior, and King T'Challa's romantic partner. Though the couple spend time apart, the turmoil surrounding T'Challa's coronation draws them back together. Nakia has a committed, adventurous spirit, often working beyond Wakanda's borders. She believes her wealthy nation should use its resources to help the world. Eventually, she convinces T'Challa of this, too.

NAKIA'S KIMOYO BEADS

Nigerian-style chador

UNDERCOVER MISSIONS

Nakia cannot hide away in her homeland while innocent people, including non-Wakandans, are oppressed in other countries. She readily volunteers for a dangerous mission to free human trafficking victims in Nigeria.

Kimoyo bead can turn cars into remote-controlled vehicles

Arms crossed in Wakandan salute

DATA FILE

> Nakia tells T'Challa that she would be a good queen because she is stubborn.

> During an undercover mission in Busan, South Korea, Nakia drives a speeding car through the city in her usual manner—in bare feet.

MASTER SPY

Nakia is a member of Wakanda's intelligence agency. She is sent on covert assignments in foreign countries as far away as South Korea, all to further the interests of her country. This includes rescuing Wakandan citizens in peril on foreign soil, as well as conducting espionage.

Green pattern reflects lush River Tribe homeland

As an important member of the River Tribe, Nakia is returned to Wakanda in a Royal Talon Fighter to attend T'Challa's Challengo Ceremony and coronation.

Despite their love for each other, Nakia and T'Challa don't always see eye to eye. Headstrong and passionate, Nakia's dedication to helping others outside Wakanda keeps her away for long periods and threatens to expose her country and its secrets. It puts Nakia at odds with T'Challa's desire to safeguard his nation through isolation—until she persuades him otherwise.

Nakia refuses to accept Killmonger as Wakanda's king after he seemingly kills T'Challa in the Challenge Ceremony. She steals a power-enhancing heart-shaped herb before the entire crop is burned, to offer to the Jabari Tribe leader, M'Baku, in return for his help in overthrowing Killmonger.

Sharp vibranium blade (energy turned off)

Activation handle

CHAKRAMS

Nakia wields two chakram blades. The deadly vibranium throwing rings can be activated to emit blasts of energy when the weapons impact their target.

Vibranium spaulder

INTO BATTLE

As a spy, Nakia is an expert in armed and unarmed combat. She uses a variety of martial arts to dispatch a number of the vibranium thief Klaue's henchmen during a mission in Busan. Later, wearing *Dora Milaje* armor and wielding dual chakrams, Nakia holds her own against Killmonger, who is clad in a Black Panther combat suit and powered by the heart-shaped herb.

Leather and vibranium patchwork leggings

SHURI

Princess Shuri is the daughter of King T'Chaka and Queen Ramonda and the sister of Prince (later King) T'Challa of Wakanda. She is brilliant, funny, and doesn't hesitate to speak her mind. She's also a highly skilled engineer and scientist, and leader of the Wakanda Design Group, which develops new uses for vibranium. T'Challa recognizes the value of Shuri's contributions and appoints her director of Wakanda's Foreign Outreach Center in California.

ROYAL SISTER

Shuri is T'Challa's younger sister and only sibling. If anything were to happen to T'Challa, she would be heir presumptive in the ensuing Challenge Ceremony. Her safety is important to the security of Wakanda for this reason, but also because of her contributions to the scientific and technological advancements of her country.

Sonic blast exits panther mouth

Paint pattern draws attention to eyes

Teeth and collar accent jawline

Lacquered vibranium finish

Vibranium armband

VIBRANIUM GAUNTLETS (FRONT VIEW)

VIBRANIUM GAUNTLETS (TOP VIEW)

Hand-painted patchwork blouse

Hand-carved buckle

Mesh fabric and leather

Stretch leggings

Skirt wrap

CEREMONIAL ROLE

It is Shuri's duty to attend the Challenge Ceremony and coronation of her brother, T'Challa. As a member of the royal family, she has the option to challenge his ascension to the throne.

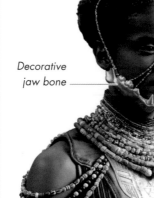

Decorative jaw bone

Strings of clay beads

Handmade ceremonial outfit

Uncomfortable traditional corset

Kimoyo beads

Vibranium ore

VIBRANIUM CANISTER

Airlock seal

Holographic communicator

Emergency medical stabilizer

TECH GENIUS

Shuri has expertise in engineering, physics, chemistry, medicine, and computer programming. She is a talented designer, too, and can craft vibranium better than anyone in Wakanda. Shuri's lab is located inside the vibranium mine. There she designs upgraded Black Panther suits, new uses for Kimoyo beads, and other gadgets. The lab also includes a high-tech medical clinic.

KIMOYO BEADS

Kimoyo beads are an advanced piece of vibranium-based technology, worn on the left wrist. Each bead is designed for a particular use, and the beads a person carries are suited to their needs. Beads can be utilized for medical needs, communication, holographic projection, remote vehicle control, and a host of other uses.

Wakanda has a whole mountain full of vibranium, which was bestowed by the impact of an asteroid in ancient times. The entire Wakandan economy is based on its extraction and utilization.

EVERETT K. ROSS

Everett K. Ross is a dutiful American CIA agent in charge of ensuring compliance with the Sokovia Accords. He is a former Armed Forces pilot and was Deputy Task Force Commander of the Joint Counter Terrorist Center in Germany, which is where he first met T'Challa. His meticulous investigation of the Battle of Sokovia uncovers a connection to Wakandan vibranium that, in turn, leads him to South African arms dealer Ulysses Klaue.

Ross meets Klaue at a secret club in Busan, South Korea. He sets up a sting operation to nab Klaue, but isn't counting on the uncouth criminal bringing so many armed guards.

ADVANCED SCIENCE

Skeptical Ross seriously underestimates Wakanda's technological advancements. He first realizes the truth when Shuri uses vibranium to save him from a lethal bullet wound in her pioneering lab. Later joining the battle against Killmonger, Everett chases down enemy planes by piloting T'Challa's personal jet remotely from the lab. Despite his trepidation, he soon grasps how to control the virtual interface, and is able to draw on his piloting experience.

Explosion of enemy target

Royal Talon jet swoops through sky, piloted remotely by Ross

OKOYE

Okoye is the leader of the *Dora Milaje*, the all-female special forces of Wakanda. She is not just T'Challa's best soldier, though—Okoye is also a close friend and confidant. She is intelligent, well educated, and highly trained in security procedures. Okoye is also multilingual, speaking her native language of Xhosa as well as English and some Korean. She can be gruff at times, but she also has a good sense of humor—and a romantic side.

Okoye pilots T'Challa's Royal Talon Fighter. The ship responds to voice commands and does not have conventional manual controls, but Shuri can configure holographic remote controls to fly them "American style" too.

Vibranium spearhead

Dora Milaje *leadership* tattoo

Gold-plated vibranium rings protect neck

Hand-stitching and beadwork

Hand-tooled, gold-plated vibranium spaulder

Connection-point to lock spears

Leather harness passed down through generations

Gold-plated bracers jingle with movement

Medallion buckle with cat face

THE GENERAL

Okoye is head of the Wakandan military and is in charge of security and intelligence. She accompanies T'Challa on his trips outside Wakanda and can be seen by his side at all formal occasions. Her loyalty is so strong that she's willing to stand against her husband, W'Kabi, to protect King T'Challa.

Kimoyo bead grants access to pilot ship

Spear can be electrified

Intricate beadwork on tabard

MASTER WARRIOR

Okoye is renowned as the country's top warrior and an unrivaled master of Wakandan martial arts. She has the responsibility of training the other *Dora Milaje*.

Activates/ deactivates nearby electronic devices

Leather boots over vibranium and leather patchwork leggings

Split-toe boots have powerful electromagnetic soles

Protective talismans

Trained to be vigilant and poised for action, Okoye patrols the upper balcony of the casino. She is the first to spy Klaue's henchmen entering the club.

Fearless in combat in any terrain, Okoye attacks Klaue's getaway car from the roof of a speeding vehicle as she and Nakia give chase through the streets of Busan.

Ill-fitting undercover wig

Decorative gold necklace

IN DISGUISE

Some security assignments require Okoye to go undercover. She joins T'Challa and Nakia at a Busan casino to apprehend the vibranium smuggler Klaue. To blend in with the gangsters and their dates she wears an evening dress and an annoying wig to conceal her conspicuous *Dora Milaje* tattoos.

Wooden purse holds compacted spears

CASINO DRESS

As leader of the *Dora Milaje*, Okoye is duty bound to serve Wakanda's king. When Killmonger defeats T'Challa, Nakia cannot persuade Okoye to leave the palace with her, Ramonda, and Shuri.

FOREIGN AFFAIRS

Okoye is never far from her king's side, especially on missions outside Wakanda. On such occasions, she keeps her discussions with T'Challa secret by speaking to him in Xhosa.

DATA FILE

> Okoye takes a dislike to CIA agent Everett K. Ross when she first meets him, telling T'Challa she will "impale him on that desk."

> Okoye is sent to locate Nakia and fetch her home for King T'Chaka's funeral. However, she is too late, and only finds Nakia in time for T'Challa's coronation.

THE *DORA MILAJE*

Fabric woven with vibranium threads

The royal guards of the king of Wakanda are known as the *Dora Milaje*. This all-female regiment of bodyguards are the fiercest, most feared warriors in the country. The *Dora Milaje* fighting style is like a choreographed dance—each carries a spear and they fight as one. In Wakanda, they wear traditional armor, but when joining the king overseas, they wear modest black outfits. They are instantly identifiable by their ceremonially shaved heads.

Intimidating royal red tabard

AYO

Wakandan law forbids anyone, including the *Dora Milaje*, from interfering in the Challenge Ceremony. Okoye, Nakia, and Ayo can only watch helplessly as Killmonger appears to kill T'Challa.

The *Dora Milaje* owe strict allegiance to the Wakandan throne. T'Challa's return negates the Challenge Ceremony's outcome, no longer binding the warriors to Killmonger. They turn on the usurper.

KILLMONGER

Erik "Killmonger" Stevens (Wakandan birth name: N'Jadaka) is motivated by revenge and a burning desire to change the world. He is the son of N'Jobu, brother of King T'Chaka of Wakanda. In 1992, N'Jobu helped the arms dealer Ulysses Klaue steal Wakandan vibranium. Shortly afterward, the king traveled to Oakland, California to confront his brother and, during the ensuing scuffle, killed him. Abandoned to his fate, the orphaned Stevens committed himself to one day claiming the throne of Wakanda, and using its advanced weapons to arm the African diaspora.

Chain holds royal ring of grandfather King Azzuri

Body armor harness

Body armor plate

Daniel Defense DDM4 MK18 assault rifle

Rifle scope

Patina on vibranium ax head

At the Museum of Great Britain, Killmonger asks the African antiquities curator about an artifact. She tells him it is a 7th century piece constructed by the Fula people. He corrects her that it is actually a vibranium artifact looted from Wakanda, and he and his gang then take it.

Grenade, ready to be thrown

Two-handed grip allows for forceful blows

SPECIAL FORCES TRAINING

Stevens trains his whole life to be a killer. At age 19, he graduates from the U.S. Naval Academy in Annapolis, and he goes on to join the Navy SEALS and serve combat tours in both Iraq and Afghanistan. Stevens is later recruited into a Joint Special Operations Command (JSOC) black-ops unit, where his extremely high kill count earns him the nickname "Killmonger." Proud of his Wakandan roots, Stevens has the tattoo of a War Dog (a member of Wakanda's intelligence agency) inside his lower lip, although he never actually trained as one.

M203A1 grenade launcher

Thigh holster

ANCIENT WAKANDAN AX

Killmonger meets his cousin T'Challa for the first time in Wakanda's throne room. He claims his right to challenge T'Challa's kingship.

Camouflage cargo pants

Killmonger's body is covered in scars; each one represents someone he has slain. He considers each kill to be training for Wakanda's Challenge Ceremony, where he will claim the throne.

Balmain military boots

KILLMONGER'S WEAPONS

Killmonger uses an ancient vibranium sword and spear to defeat T'Challa at the Warrior Falls Challenge Ceremony, breaking off the spear's shaft to transform it into a dagger. Proud of his accomplishments, Killmonger keeps these weapons as trophies, wielding them again when T'Challa returns to challenge him.

Ornate ceremonial spearhead

Gold particles infuse suit

Decorative ears with audio booster

Lines act as kinetic energy absorbers

Snarling decoration designed to intimidate opponents

Sworn to protect the throne, the *Dora Milaje* turn against Killmonger when they discover that T'Challa is still alive and that Killmonger's challenge was unsuccessful.

Blade shape designed for cutting rather than piercing

Entire suit can compress into necklace

HERITAGE RECLAIMED

When Killmonger arrives in Wakanda, he reclaims his own Wakandan birth name, N'Jadaka. He deposes T'Challa as king, before taking the heart-shaped herb for himself and becoming a Black Panther. N'Jadaka then dons an advanced Black Panther suit originally created for T'Challa by Shuri.

LEAF-SHAPED SWORD

As a pure fighter, Killmonger's skills exceed T'Challa's. T'Challa has to use his strategic mind and extensive knowledge of Wakanda to defeat him.

Gold-plated vibranium belt

SPEAR

DATA FILE

> Killmonger steals a Dogon mask from the Museum of Great Britain. The Dogon wear them in funeral masquerades, called damas.

> Killmonger gains the loyalty of T'Challa's friend W'Kabi by giving him the body of Ulysses Klaue, who killed W'Kabi's father.

Extendable vibranium claws

153

DOCTOR STRANGE

The world is not as it first appears. There is another, stranger world, hidden from this one. In that world, reality can be folded as easily as paper, and people can transport themselves from one corner of the Earth to another as easily as flicking a switch. It is also a dangerous world, full of dark forces and evil entities. All that stands between it and our own is an order of powerful sorcerers: the Masters of the Mystic Arts. Their mysterious leader, sworn to protect Earth at all costs, is Doctor Strange.

"DORMAMMU, I'VE COME TO BARGAIN!"

DOCTOR STRANGE

Renowned New York neurosurgeon Stephen Strange M.D., Ph.D. is at the peak of his career when a horrific car accident leaves his hands maimed and brings his whole world to a screeching halt. The egotistical Doctor Strange is frustrated when repeated surgeries fail to restore the use of his hands. He loses his career and everything he cares about, before traveling to Nepal to find a mysterious temple known as Kamar-Taj, hoping to find the healing there that has thus far eluded him.

DOCTOR CHRISTINE PALMER

Christine Palmer is Strange's colleague and girlfriend. She is kind and compassionate, taking care of him through his accident and recovery. Yet he pushes her away, and when his toxic words are too much, Christine leaves him—though she later helps Strange when he needs her most.

Inscription from Christine

Hair covered for operation

Before his accident, Strange has no semblance of humility. He plays musical games during surgery to keep himself from getting bored, and delights in humiliating colleagues that he considers less capable.

MASTER SURGEON

Strange is in very high demand as a surgeon, allowing him to pick and choose who to operate on. He only selects high-profile patients with a strong chance of recovery, to prevent his perfect record being tarnished. But Strange's fame leads to his downfall. On his way to speak at a Neurological Society dinner, a collision sends his car off a cliff.

Disposable surgical mask

Strange lives in an ostentatious high-rise apartment. A grand piano sits across from a cabinet full of his awards.

STRANGE'S WATCH

Hands up to avoid contamination

STRANGE'S INJURIES

It takes so long for rescuers to locate Strange's car that his hands suffer severe, permanent nerve damage. He undergoes eleven hours of surgery and receives stainless steel pins in the bones of both hands. Strange endures a total of seven successive surgeries, but his doctors are unable to restore his normal hand function.

Fixator pin support system

Arm brace

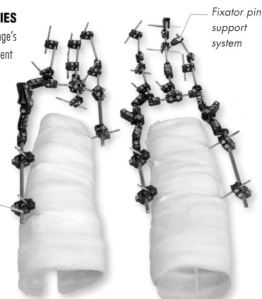

Strange's physical therapist tells him about a man named Jonathan Pangborn, who recovered from injuries that were even worse than Strange's.

FINGER PINS

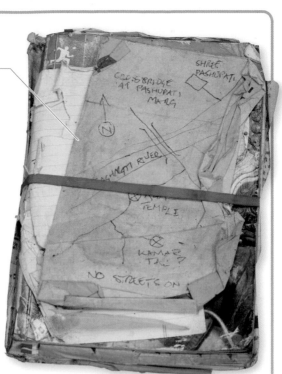

Bedraggled hair

Scruffy beard

Hand-drawn map of Kathmandu

A DESPERATE SEARCH

Stephen Strange uses nearly all of his finances on unsuccessful surgeries after his horrible car accident. After meeting former paraplegic Jonathan Pangborn and hearing his story about being miraculously healed at Kamar-Taj, Strange redirects his efforts. He uses what little money he has left to fly to Nepal and search Kathmandu for Kamar-Taj. Without any real idea where to go or understanding of the local language, he wanders aimlessly for days.

Water-resistant canvas

SKETCH MAPS AND GUIDES

FINDING KAMAR-TAJ

Apart from the clothes he is wearing, everything Strange now owns fits inside his backpack. He has a handful of guidebooks, notes, and maps to navigate, but he still manages to meander down dangerous alleys. Strange eats and sleeps on the street, falling victim to numerous scams and robberies.

Bridle leather straps

TRAVELER'S RUCKSACK

Layered clothing for changing weather

Strange mistakenly assumes Kamar-Taj will be a traditional Nepalese religious retreat, and searches local holy sites like the Swayambhunath Temple on a hill to the west of Kathmandu, and the Krishna Mandir Temple in Lalitpur (seen left). He is on the verge of despair when the sorcerer Master Mordo finds him and brings him to Kamar-Taj.

After introducing him to the Multiverse, The Ancient One throws Strange out of Kamar-Taj. She is afraid that his arrogance will lead him down the same dark path as her rogue protégé Kaecilius, and wants to test Strange's commitment—a test that ultimately he passes.

DOCTOR STRANGE:
MASTER OF THE MYSTIC ARTS

As a student of the Mystic Arts, Stephen Strange is adept at self-study. Powered with a photographic memory and Google Translate, he rapidly reads his way through the library of Kamar-Taj. He even studies in his astral body while his physical body rests. His skills leap forward and he finds a new ally in the form of the Cloak of Levitation. Strange finally proves himself a true Master of the Mystic Arts by confronting the fallen Master Kaecilius and then vanquishing the interdimensional villain Dormammu.

At first, novice student Strange stalls in his progress during training, struggling to surrender to The Ancient One's illogical teachings. Acceptance brings improvement and soon leads to greatness.

Conjured shield

Eye of Agamotto

Cloak of Levitation

Braided belt with sling ring

EARTH'S GUARDIAN

Following the death of The Ancient One and the defeat of Kaecilius and Dormammu, Doctor Strange assumes the role of Master of the New York Sanctum. He keeps a watch list of individuals and beings from other realms who may be a threat, and assists the Avengers in keeping the world safe.

Bridge

DOCTOR STRANGE'S SLING RING

Finger holes

Hand wearing sling ring

SLING RINGS

Sling rings are a magical device worn by sorcerers on the second and third digits of their left hand. The left hand is held high while the right hand spins counterclockwise to conjure a gateway to another dimension, or other place visualized by the sorcerer. Each ring is uniquely crafted.

Cloak takes up defensive posture

Boot straps keep footwear secure during flight

Bronze front cover

Central conduit for magical energy

Eye of Agamotto diagram

Time manipulation instructions

BOOK OF CAGLIOSTRO

The Ancient One has a private collection of advanced magic books within the library of Kamar-Taj. Among them is the *Book of Cagliostro*, which contains instructions for the Eye of Agamotto, as well as spells to access the dreaded Dark Dimension.

Before it can be used, the Eye of Agamotto must be opened. This requires a series of hand motions detailed in the *Book of Cagliostro*.

EYE OF AGAMOTTO

The first Sorcerer Supreme was Agamotto, and he created the Eye that bears his name. The Eye's magical green-glowing center is the Time Stone, one of several vastly powerful Infinity Stones sought by the Mad Titan Thanos. Tampering with the Eye is extremely dangerous. It can cause branches in time, unstable dimensional openings, spatial paradoxes, and time loops. It can even erase an unwitting user from existence.

Gheri cotton and leather strap

Runes carved in gold plating

Chamber for the Time Stone

Decorative gold clasps with ruby inlay

Layered Japanese wool with embroidered edges

Case allows wielder to use Time Stone without physically touching it

The Eye of Agamotto has the power to reverse the effects of time, or advance them into any number of future possibilities. Even a being as mighty as Dormammu is helpless against it.

Printed checkered inner lining

CLOAK OF LEVITATION

The Cloak of Levitation is a sentient magical relic that floats in a glass case in the New York Sanctum—until it meets Doctor Strange. Renowned for being extremely fickle, for some reason it is drawn to Strange. It not only allows him to fly, but also anticipates dangers; pulling Strange away from threats whether he approves or not.

THE ANCIENT ONE

The Ancient One is an unrivaled Master of the Mystic Arts, sworn to defend Earth from supernatural threats. Her origins are shrouded in mystery, but unknown to her students, she maintains her unnaturally long life by drawing magical energy from the forbidden Dark Dimension. She buys this time to train sorcerers who can share her dangerous mission. Some of her efforts have failed disastrously, and those students have gone down evil paths. The Ancient One trains Doctor Strange to be her successor as the next Sorcerer Supreme, just before she is killed by her former protégé, Kaecilius.

Head shaved to shun distracting vanities

Timeless clothing cannot be identified with particular era

Wide black sash contrasts with yellow hue

Decorative scarfs can be weaponized with magic

The barriers of time and space are meaningless to sorcerers. The Ancient One may be visiting a Tibetan teahouse one moment and chasing rogue sorcerers through the streets of London in the next.

SORCERER SUPREME

The Ancient One's followers know very little about her, other than the fact that she is Celtic and centuries old. For whatever reason, she never speaks of her own past. The title of Sorcerer Supreme has been passed down for thousands of years, beginning with the first Sorcerer Supreme, Agamotto. She has followed Stephen Strange's life for a long time prior to his arrival at Kamar-Taj.

Warm woolen underskirt for chilly Nepalese weather

The Ancient One's private classroom has a beautiful dark wooden interior with ornately carved pillars. Fragrant incense wafts through the air while tea services sit on low tables.

Occasionally The Ancient One must shock students to make her point understood. She pushes Strange's astral form outside his body and into the Astral Dimension—a place where sorcerers can travel separate from their physical form.

Feet tilted downward during levitation

KAMAR-TAJ

The Ancient One resides in Kamar-Taj, a learning center hidden in Kathmandu, Nepal. Here she teaches students in the Mystic Arts. Kamar-Taj houses an extensive library of mystical texts, a collection of magical relics, lodgings, and training facilities. It is linked via portals to three Sanctums, in Hong Kong, New York, and London.

The Ancient One is a skilled teacher. She has tutored students for centuries and is adept at tailoring her lessons to each student. In Strange's case, she explains that it might help him to think of spells in scientific terms; like a program to alter the source code of reality.

THE MYSTIC ARTS

Sorcerers harness energy from other dimensions, using it to create weapons, shields, and gateways. Distracted by his injuries, Strange has difficulty learning these basics. The Ancient One tells Strange that he can't always force things to happen the way he wants. She helps him learn by transporting him to Mount Everest, where he has just two minutes to make a magical gateway and escape before the cold sends him into shock.

A successful gateway causes a fold in spacetime, allowing sorcerers to travel between two places instantaneously.

Summit of
Mount Everest

Magical
energy glows
orange

DATA FILE

> The Ancient One carries a small wooden fan. This magical relic enhances her ability to conjure weapons that function like Japanese war fans.

> Her centuries of life have made The Ancient One a skilled linguist. She can read and speak many languages, including some that are long lost to history.

She may be old and powerful, but The Ancient One is also human. She doesn't want to face death alone. She bares her soul and imparts vital wisdom to Strange in her final moments, stretching her time out as long as she can.

MASTER MORDO

Mordo came to Kamar-Taj looking for power and a means for revenge. Yet under the tutelage of The Ancient One, Mordo believes he has found inner peace and a life centered on the laws of nature. He becomes an accomplished sorcerer, but The Ancient One believes his approach to magic is too rigid, and thinks he and Steven Strange can balance each other. When Mordo discovers that The Ancient One has prolonged her own life by drawing on the forbidden power of the Dark Dimension, he loses heart and abandons his fellow sorcerers.

Staff's impact sends opponents flying

Intricate layering mirrors complex psyche

Hand ready to punch or cast spell

Comfortable yak wool top

Ornate handmade leather belt

Handles at each end pull apart

Segments separate, revealing magical energy inside

Mordo hears Stephen Strange asking people about Kamar-Taj as he wanders the streets of Kathmandu. He shows compassion by aiding Strange when he is mugged in an alleyway, but also demonstrates his propensity for solving problems by using violence.

A DARK PATH

Mordo has a great deal of faith in The Ancient One and her teachings. When he discovers she has broken her own rules, his confidence turns to self-righteousness and indignation. Once a devoted Master of the Mystic Arts, he turns against the order, accusing it of meddling with nature's laws. He comes to believe that he alone is worthy to wield the Mystic Arts.

Mordo takes an active role in teaching students the Mystic Arts, though his instruction lacks the tranquility of The Ancient One. His teachings emphasize urgency and the need to be ready for potentially lethal encounters.

STAFF OF THE LIVING TRIBUNAL

Mordo's staff is said to have belonged to a cosmic entity known for exacting impartial yet brutal judgments. The volatile orange energy inside allows it to transform and be used as a whip or flail.

DATA FILE

> Mordo's hooded cloak hides his identity from his enemies when he roams outside of Kamar-Taj. In a more figurative sense, it also conceals his conflicted mind.

> The Ancient One sensed Mordo's overconfidence and judgmental nature. She warned him that his temptations toward darker impulses would never cease, but thought he could rise above them.

Vaulting Boots of Valtorr let Mordo defy gravity

Mordo does not respect Doctor Strange's abilities or his commitment. He accuses Strange of being a spineless coward for his unwillingness to kill for their cause. In his accusations, Mordo betrays that he has committed dark deeds as a sorcerer.

MASTER WONG

Wong is the newest librarian at Kamar-Taj, installed after his predecessor was murdered by renegade Kaecilius and his Zealots. His duties are important—he guides the studies and extracurricular reading of students. He also curates Kamar-Taj's collection of magical relics and aids in the defense against mystical forces. Wong is killed defending the Hong Kong sanctum, but restored to life when Doctor Strange uses the Eye of Agamotto to reverse time, restore the Sanctum, and defeat Kaecilius and Dormammu.

Stern gaze hides dark sense of humor

Subdued maroon robes compliment solemn demeanor

Strange absorbs the contents of the library extremely quickly. Seeing this, Wong lets him access books intended for advanced, Master-level students.

NEW LIBRARIAN

Wong takes his librarian duties seriously. He warns Strange that the penalty for removing books from Kamar-Taj is death! Despite his serious nature, Wong is helpful in recommending books for Strange to study. Nobody knows the library's contents better than Wong—except perhaps The Ancient One.

Curious about Strange's frequent musical references, Wong discovers a new taste for Western pop. Although it is against the rules to conjure gateways in the library and circumvent Wong's oversight, Wong is too distracted by the music to notice Strange sneaking in to "borrow" books about astral projection.

WAND OF WATOOMB

Wong's Wand of Watoomb is a magical baton with a horned head on each end. The wand can be used to wield energy; usually by absorbing, amplifying, and redirecting it.

Faces glow when in use

Magically insulated stand

Leather of unknown, non-bovine origin

BOOK OF THE INVISIBLE SUN

ASTRONOMIA NOVA

CODEX IMPERIUM

MAXIM'S PRIMER

SANCTUMS

The three Sanctums are treasure houses of magical relics and bases for Masters of the Mystic Arts. Most importantly, their radiating magic forms a shield around the Earth, protecting it from incursions by evil forces from other dimensions. Located in New York, London, and Hong Kong, the Sanctums are targeted by the rogue sorcerer Kaecilius. He plans to destroy them and allow the demon Dormammu and his Dark Dimension to invade Earth. After Doctor Strange successfully fends off Dormammu, he takes up residence in the New York Sanctum as its new Master.

The New York Sanctum occupies a large building, with a circular window as its most striking feature. It would garner more attention from residents of New York City, were it not for spells that keep passersby moving along. Still, notable guests like Thor and Loki do stop by from time to time.

ORB OF AGAMOTTO

The levitating Orb of Agamotto is kept in the library antechamber of Kamar-Taj seminary. It allows The Ancient One to monitor the integrity of the shield radiated by each Sanctum. The Orb was created by Earth's first Sorcerer Supreme, Agamotto, and it is said that its magical power is still drawn from Agamotto himself.

New York Sanctum's shield

Hong Kong Sanctum's shield

London Sanctum's shield

Panels of wood not of this Earth

"Window of the Worlds" protects the Sanctum from mystical invaders

Doctor Strange ponders his destiny

Parquet hardwood floor from European castle

Cabinet full of dried ingredients

Iron guardians occasionally animate

NEW YORK SANCTUM

The New York Sanctum is located at 177A Bleecker Street in Greenwich Village, New York. It is an elegant residence, complete with a library, Chamber of Relics, Rotunda of Gateways linking to various locations around the world, and a seemingly endless labyrinth of rooms yet to be discovered. The Sanctum's interior is larger than its outer dimensions suggest.

DAGGER OF DAVAROTH

One of Davaroth's many heads

"Davaroth's pointy sting"

MITIGATOR OF MINH MANG

CHAMBER OF RELICS

The New York Sanctum has an impressive exhibit of ancient magical relics. Here, Doctor Strange first encounters the Cloak of Levitation. Other relics include the Hoary Hosts of Hoggoth, the Daggers of Davaroth, and the Pincers of Power.

The New York Sanctum has a luxurious entryway with imported tile floors and a majestic curved staircase. It is the scene of Doctor Strange's first encounter with Kaecilius and his Zealots.

Tribal wraps from the tropics

Sling ring secured on large woven belt

Golden Gauntlets of Gamorr

DEFENDING NEW YORK

When Kaecilius attacks the New York Sanctum, its Master, Daniel Drumm, bravely attempts to defend it, but is quickly overpowered. Doctor Strange rushes to stop Kaecilius, but it is apparent that he is out of his depth. Strange stumbles through the Chamber of Relics, hurling obscure magical items at Kaecilius, though he has no idea how to use them.

Scratchy neck shackle

Pinchy arm restrictor

Uncomfortable torso brace restraint

The Specter's Staff

The Cloak of Levitation helps Strange save the New York Sanctum by pointing him toward the Crimson Bands of Cyttorak. This magical metal ribcage snaps around Kaecilius' body, briefly immobilizing him.

Squeezing waist clasper

CRIMSON BANDS OF CYTTORAK

MASTER DANIEL DRUMM

HONG KONG SANCTUM

The Hong Kong Sanctum is Kaecilius' third and final target in his quest to usher in the arrival of Dormammu. The Sanctum is situated in a modern building in a busy Kowloon neighborhood, among a sea of neon signs and high-rise buildings. Kaecilius succeeds in destroying the Sanctum and killing those protecting it, but Strange uses the Eye of Agamotto to reverse time, repairing it and bringing its defenders back to life.

Hong Kong skyscraper engulfed by dimensional rift

Center of Dark Dimensional incursion

Strange arrives at the Hong Kong Sanctum after the battle has already been lost by his fellow sorcerers. The Sanctum is in flames and the surrounding streets lie in rubble.

THE MULTIVERSE

The world that Doctor Strange knows is just one of an infinite number of realities known as dimensions. Some, like our own, are pleasant and inviting. Other dimensions are inhospitable, dark, and evil. Malevolent beings from those realms seek to conquer and consume the other realities in the Multiverse. Sorcerers are able to visit some of these realms through an intermediary Astral Dimension, which allows their souls to travel while separated from their bodies. Masters of the Mystic Arts can also employ sling rings to open gateways and visit other dimensions using their physical bodies. Yet some dimensions are so malignant and terrifying that they must be sealed off at all costs.

Doctor Strange's introduction to the Multiverse is unsettling. While in his astral body and under the direction of The Ancient One, he warps through endless converging possibilities.

ACTINIARIA DIMENSION

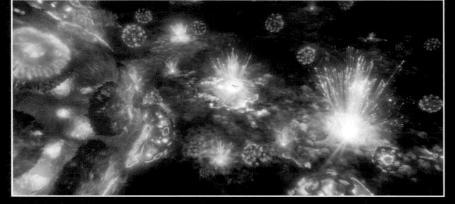

FLOWERING INCENSE DIMENSION

GRASS JELLY DIMENSION

INFINITE DIMENSIONS

Not even The Ancient One has seen all of the dimensions in the Multiverse. One could spend an entire lifetime traveling and still not explore a significant selection of them. Known dimensions include paradoxes like the Quantum Realm where size is diminished infinitely, the Realm of Madness, the Actiniaria and Mandelibus dimensions, and the Quadriverse. Some dimensions are full of life, with intelligent beings and magnificent cultures. Others, like the Grass Jelly and Flowering Incense dimensions, are uninhabitable and can only be visited in astral form.

MANDELIBUS DIMENSION

DATA FILE

> The Mandelibus Dimension contains human hands that endlessly branch like fractals. Though many appear to be copies, some seem to have a mind of their own.

> The Mandelibus Dimension gives Doctor Strange nightmares. As a consequence, he decides never to visit a new dimension without researching it first.

MIRROR DIMENSION

The Mirror Dimension is a parallel reality used by sorcerers to practice magic without affecting their own. The barrier between the real world and the Mirror Dimension appears like a wall of shattered glass. No known life originates in the Mirror Dimension—it is only an empty reflection.

Mirror buildings twist as easily as paper

In theory, there are no limits to what magic can achieve in the Mirror Dimension. The whole world can be folded in upon itself. However, a sorcerer can still be killed here, or locked inside if they lose their sling ring.

DARK DIMENSION

The Dark Dimension exists in a void of time and the laws of physics. Any light there is cold; it can be seen, yet it does not radiate energy. The Dark Dimension is a corruption of the original reality that was once found there, and an amalgamation of countless other dimensions that its master, Dormammu, has consumed.

Cloud of corrupted collective memories

Formerly inhabited world

Sound waves transmuted into a tangible substance

Dormammu's ancient essence has been altered so many times by the assimilation of other universes that his original form and his own primordial dimension are long forgotten.

KAECILIUS

Kaecilius is a broken man who has lost everything when he first arrives at the mystic seminary Kamar-Taj. He studies under The Ancient One, who senses that he is stubborn, ambitious, and aggressive, but also unusually gifted in the Mystic Arts. His skills develop and he trains others, but all the while he is haunted by his family's ghosts and longs to defeat death itself. He tries to find a way to change his past and learns of the *Book of Cagliostro*. When he discovers that The Ancient One uses it to draw power from the Dark Dimension, but will not share the knowledge for extending life, Kaecilius is enraged and resolves to take the knowledge for himself.

After losing his son in an accident, Kaecilius suffers a second blow when his wife Adria is taken by a sudden illness. Distraught and suicidal, he drowns his sadness in alcohol. Mordo finds Kaecilius in Denmark and brings him to Kamar-Taj. There The Ancient One promises him enlightenment and a means to find peace.

After he contacts Dormammu, Kaecilius' already formidable skills are boosted by energy flowing from the Dark Dimension. He is able to deflect Doctor Strange's magical attacks without difficulty.

Symbol of Dormammu

Hair pulled back for fighting

Dark Dimensional energy leaching through eyes

Sleeveless cloak designed for close combat

Conjured spear of fractured spacetime

Inlaid Tibetan belt

Magical blade can slice through flesh with ease

Boot covers for cold, rainy environment

Large inner pockets for stolen relics

Heavy blade balanced by large pommel

SCYTHE DAGGERS
Kaecilius carries a pair of gruesome daggers behind his back, in the folds of his cloak. Their grisly form is emblematic of his disregard for human life.

DISCIPLE OF DORMAMMU

For Kaecilius, time is the ultimate enemy, as time inevitably leads to death. He seeks the eternal life promised by Dormammu in the Dark Dimension, where time does not exist. Kaecilius strikes a deal with Dormammu, offering him access to Earth and its universe in exchange for perpetual life. Too late, Kaecilius discovers that the "immortality" Dormammu offers is actually an everlasting torment.

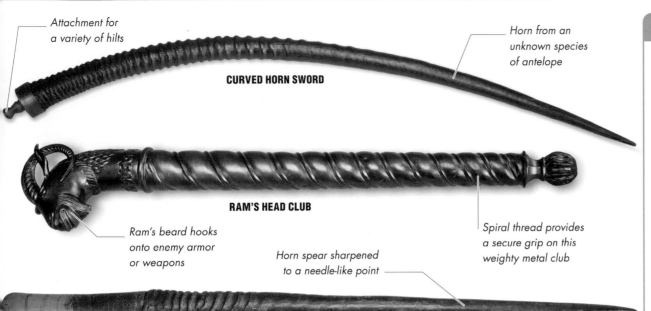

Attachment for
a variety of hilts

CURVED HORN SWORD

Horn from an
unknown species
of antelope

RAM'S HEAD CLUB

Ram's beard hooks
onto enemy armor
or weapons

Horn spear sharpened
to a needle-like point

Spiral thread provides
a secure grip on this
weighty metal club

SPEAR OF SEVERITY

DATA FILE

> Energy drawn from the Dark Dimension is amplified in the Mirror Dimension, making Kaecilius even more powerful there.

> Matter, gravity, and the laws of physics are all folded in the Mirror Dimension, allowing sorcerers to walk on walls and ceilings.

> Kaecilius acquires the ability to fold matter outside the Mirror Dimension, which is very dangerous and demonstrates great power.

ZEALOT WEAPONS

Kaecilius' followers or "Zealots" are adept in martial arts and can use even non-magical weapons in multiple ways. The ram's head club, for example, can be used as a cudgel, a throwing missile, or a hook to whisk enemies' weapons out of their hands. Weapons adapted from animal horns are a favorite—the unfortunate beasts having been sacrificed in obscure Zealot rituals.

Kaecilius manipulates the discontent of his students at Kamar-Taj to turn them against The Ancient One. He promises to teach them all they desire, but he is only using his Zealots to reach Dormammu.

DORMAMMU: DESTROYER OF WORLDS

Dormammu is an immensely powerful extradimensional being and master of the Dark Dimension. He is ravenous for power and seeks to devour all other dimensions in the Multiverse. In a desperate attempt to stop him consuming Earth, Doctor Strange uses the Eye of Agamotto to introduce time into the Dark Dimension, imprisoning Dormammu in an endless loop in which he kills Strange again and again. Dormammu agrees to leave Earth forever to regain his freedom, taking Kaecilius and his Zealots with him.

Spells to open
dimensional rift

Symbol of
Dormammu

THE STOLEN PAGES

Kaecilius and his students sneak into the library of Kamar-Taj, murder the librarian, and steal two pages from the *Book of Cagliostro*. The spells contained on the pages allow them to draw power from the Dark Dimension and communicate with Dormammu.

Unaware that the dire warnings for the spells he has stolen are located on later pages, Kaecilius remains in ignorance of his horrifying fate.

GUARDIANS OF THE GALAXY

Far from Earth's troubles, the rest of the universe goes about its business. Across countless worlds, wars are fought, civilizations collapse, criminals cheat and steal, and brave heroes try to stop them. Against this vast and constantly changing cosmic backdrop, a bizarre crew of outlaws, renegades, and misfits sell their skills to the highest bidder. They call themselves the Guardians of the Galaxy.

STAR-LORD

Peter Jason Quill is a galactic fortune hunter, thief, and self-styled Star-Lord. Half-Terran, half-Celestial, Quill was abducted from Earth as a child and secretly raised by the Ravagers, a notorious syndicate of space pirates. Easy-going, resourceful, and daring, he embarks on his own lucrative solo criminal career. However, when the universe comes under threat, he realizes his destiny lies as the leader of an unlikely team of interstellar adventurers-for-hire known as the Guardians of the Galaxy.

Sheer cunning, audacity, and Ravager training help Quill elude the mercenary Korath the Pursuer and his squad of Sakaaran soldiers sent to retrieve the Orb for the Kree warlord Ronan. With the much sought-after Orb in his possession, Quill becomes a marked man.

"LEGENDARY" OUTLAW

Quill's misspent youth with the Ravagers has helped him acquire expert skills in hand-to-hand combat, marksmanship, acrobatics, starship piloting, and thieving. Taking the nickname his mother Meredith gave him, he calls himself the "legendary" Star-Lord, much to the amusement of others who have either never heard of him or mistakenly refer to him as "Star-Prince" or "Space-Lord."

Quadblaster primed and ready to fire

Well-worn leather Ravagers jacket

Much-loved micro-weave T-shirt

Stab-resistant mesh patches

Belt contains pickpocketing tools

Quadblaster holster

Jet boot controls

QUADBLASTERS

Star-Lord's main offensive weapons are his Quadblasters—dual-barreled, twin-blaster handguns. The top barrel delivers a killing blast powerful enough to send a target flying through the air. The bottom barrel emits a streak of electrical energy to incapacitate a target.

Fires lethal blasts

Both barrels can be fired simultaneously

Dual triggers for index finger (top barrel) and middle finger (lower barrel)

Emits non-lethal electrical energy

QUADBLASTER

THE ORB

Hidden in an ancient temple on the deserted planet Morag is the Orb, an arcane and highly coveted artifact. Those seeking it include: Ronan the Accuser and his enforcers; the Ravagers on commission to a dealer known as the Broker; Gamora for a secret wealthy buyer; and Quill, out to sell it to the highest bidder.

Quill deploys the smarts, stealth, and equipment he picked up in his 26 years with the Ravagers to betray his former benefactors and steal the Orb for himself. Unknown to Quill, the Orb actually contains one of the mighty Infinity Stones.

Metal casing allows Quill to snare the Orb with a gravity mine

HOLO-MAP PROJECTOR

This device projects holographic historical records, mapping past structures and activities onto present reality. Quill uses it in the ruins of Morag's main city to locate the Orb inside a long-abandoned temple.

Emitter projects virtual blue holo-maps

QUILL'S MUSIC

Quill's most precious possessions are two mixtapes his mother recorded for him when he was a boy. On his ship, the *Milano*, he plays these audio cassettes on a handcrafted vintage tape deck integrated into the ship's sound system.

Vintage cassette tape deck

Awesome Mix Vol. 2 mixtape

LEADING THE GUARDIANS

Quill reveals himself to be a natural leader when he inspires the Guardians to unite as a team to defend the planet Xandar from Ronan and his superior Sakaaran forces. Giving them roles that play to their strengths, it is a far cry from their initial coming together as an unruly band of inmates trying to escape from the intergalactic prison the Kyln.

Gamora joins the showdown with Ronan

Hadron Enforcer can shatter moons

Drax provides backup

COURAGE UNDER FIRE

After Rocket's powerful Hadron Enforcer fails to stop an Infinity Stone-empowered Ronan, Quill's ingenuity, bravery, and selfless example save the day. His impromptu dance distracts Ronan, allowing Rocket to shatter the villain's hammer, which holds the Stone. Quill's superb reflexes and agility enable him to grab the Stone and, linking hands with his comrades, they use its power to vanquish Ronan.

STAR-LORD: SAVING THE UNIVERSE

His astonishing ability to hold an Infinity Stone without it destroying him makes Peter Quill a person of interest across the galaxy. The revelation that he is only half-Terran also rekindles Peter's burning desire to find out more about his father "from the stars." When his father finally appears, in the deceptive and immensely powerful form of the Celestial known as Ego, their biological bond unlocks Quill's own latent cosmic powers.

Helmet's HUD threat detection system improves wearer's reflex time

Reinforced padding

T-shirt displays alien glyphs

Built-in communications link

Heads-up display (HUD) enables thermal and ultraviolet vision

Air pressure regulators

Backup oxygen supply

Air purifier

STAR-LORD'S HELMET

Peter Quill's expanding helmet is activated by an earpiece behind his right ear. It offers a suite of life-support functions that allow him to breathe in alien atmospheres, provides ballistic protection, and boasts a heads-up display synced into his scanners, weapons, and flight systems.

CELESTIAL DEFENDER

Quill's breezy charisma, instinctive optimism, and (mostly) steadfast faith in himself and his teammates makes him a born leader. When Ego reveals Peter's true birthright to him, he releases far greater abilities within Star-Lord—the powers of a god. Like his father, Quill is immortal and invulnerable, and can manipulate matter and energy—as long as the Celestial light within Ego's planet burns.

Quill's strategic skills help the Guardians successfully defend the alien Sovereign's Anulax batteries from the interdimensional, battery-feeding Abilisk.

THE *MILANO*

Star-Lord's customized Ravager M-Ship, the *Milano*, is a versatile starship built for space flight, scavenging, personnel transport, and combat. Named after Quill's boyhood crush on the 1980s actor and singer Alyssa Milano, the ship has been extensively repaired and refitted over the years. After Quill leaves the Ravagers, the ship becomes his home—a "filthy" one according to fellow Guardian Gamora.

At the helm of the *Milano* since he was ten years old, Quill is an expert, if cocky, pilot. Fearless in the Battle of Xandar, he later flies through a perilous quantum asteroid field while evading the Sovereign's fleet of Omnicraft fighters.

Pursuing fleet of Sovereign Omnicraft

Quill and Rocket at the Milano's controls

Activation button

Proximity sensor activates next to target

Shell releases energy cord, binding target's legs

ENERGY BOLA

Quill's need for a father figure erodes his judgment, making him vulnerable to Ego's manipulation. Despite his deep, unspoken feelings for Gamora, he rejects her growing suspicions about Ego's impossibly idyllic world and his grand plans for his son.

DATA FILE

> Aside from his custom-built helmet, Star-Lord uses various high-tech equipment, such as jet boot attachments, energy bolas, a translator implant, and a gravity mine.

> Star-Lord's most treasured device is his 1980 Sony TPS-L2 Walkman cassette player.

FATHER KNOWS BEST

Having spent a lifetime wondering about his birth father, Quill's sharp instincts at first make him wary of Ego. However, once on the Celestial's planet, Peter is beguiled by his host's charm offensive and his own cosmic heritage. They blind him to Ego's true nature, but when Ego explains how he took Quill's mother's life, Peter turns on his father with fury.

Trusting expression

Ego models his look and manner on Quill

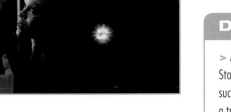

As Ego's planet crumbles below them, the Ravager Yondu jets into space with Quill, attaching his holographic spacesuit to him. By sacrificing his own life to save Star-Lord, Yondu proves that he was the real father Peter had yearned for all along.

YONDU

Yondu Udonta leads a key faction of the galactic pirates known as the Ravagers. Ruthless and cunning, he breaks the Ravagers' code by kidnapping children for the power-mad Celestial Ego, and is exiled from the group. Later, beset with guilt, he atones for his actions by helping destroy Ego and sacrificing himself to save his adopted, son Peter Quill.

Yondu is an expert pilot with excellent leadership skills. During the Battle of Xandar, he leads his Ravager M-Ships against Ronan's *Dark Aster* warship and an armada of Necrocraft fighters. He survives a brutal dogfight, flying his damaged ship to safety.

SPACE PIRATE

Yondu exhibits all the skills and lack of scruples necessary for a successful pirate captain. Smart, brave, and greedy, the Centaurian is a master thief with his eye always on the prize. Yet behind his gruff blue exterior and menacing manner is an honorable man. Fiercely loyal to his crew, he protects a young Quill by raising him as a Ravager rather than handing him over to Ego.

Yaka arrow controller converts Yondu's whistling into precise control signals

YAKA ARROW

Yondu's trademark weapon is a deadly sonically-controlled Yaka arrow. Responding to the pitch of Yondu's whistle, the self-propelled, super-fast projectile can penetrate body armor and spaceship hulls before returning to him. Its deadly power is demonstrated when Yondu uses it to wipe out his entire mutinous crew in a matter of minutes.

Red Centaurian eyes possess superior vision

Yaka metal fletching vanes give stability and pinpoint accuracy

Weathered Ravager long coat

Ravagers' universally recognized flame symbol

Shaft can burst into flame with a change of pitch

Explosive arrow tips

Yaka arrow

Armor-piercing head

Quick-draw dagger

Counterfeit Orb given to Yondu by Quill

MIRRORED PASTS

As a baby, Yondu's parents sold him to the Kree Empire, where he spent 20 years as a battle slave. It taught him to be self-reliant and resilient, refusing to let anyone get too close in case he got hurt again. He sees something of himself in Rocket, whose tough-guy act doesn't fool him. Rocket's scientific creators cared as little for their creation as Yondu's parents did for their son.

Prototype Yaka arrow control fin

After learning the terrible fate of the children he abducted for Ego, Yondu is haunted by shame. He finally redeems himself, helping the Guardians destroy the deranged Celestial and saving the life of his "son," Peter Quill, at the expense of his own.

Yondu's ultimate sacrifice is honored by his former "family" of thieves, with a beautiful and moving Ravager funeral. As Yondu's ashes drift into space, the shape of the dust appears to form an arrow.

THE RAVAGERS

The Ravagers are an interstellar crime syndicate made up of pirates, mercenaries, and assorted lawbreakers. Boasting 100 factions, its motley crews are drawn from several alien races, all wearing the Ravagers flame insignia and bound by the Ravagers code. Each faction takes its captain's name, many of whom have become legendary, such as Stakar and Aleta Ogord, Charlie-27, Krugarr, and Yondu.

Ravager uniform

All factions must adhere to the Ravagers code or face exile. On the planet Contraxia, an exiled Yondu is acutely reminded of this by Stakar Ogord's faction. By kidnapping children for Ego, when he was young and foolish, he broke the strict code—and his fellow Ravagers' hearts.

KRAGLIN OBFONTERI

Kraglin is Yondu's first mate in his breakaway Ravager faction. Staunchly devoted to his captain, he helps mentor the young Quill and stands by Yondu after many of his crew mutiny. An adept pilot, Kraglin helms the *Eclector's* Quadrant 3 starship on a successful mission to rescue the Guardians from Ego.

THE *ECLECTOR*

Each Ravager faction designs and builds its own mothership. Yondu's colossal warship, *Eclector*, is home to a crew of 100 or more, carries a full fleet of M-Ships, can deploy formidable firepower, and has detachable, armed quadrants capable of hyperspace travel.

Modular hull

Bridge

Forward floodlights

Engineering control room

Quadrant 3

Sensors

Yondu Ravager faction markings

Hyperdrive nacelle

GAMORA

Gamora is the deadliest woman in the Galaxy. When she was just a child, the despot Thanos killed half the population of her home planet, but spared Gamora's life and raised her. Trained by Thanos, alongside her adopted sister Nebula, Gamora was turned into an assassin without equal. Her fierce survival instinct, fearless fighting skills, shrewd intellect, and extensive cybernetic enhancements make her a formidable foe and an indispensable, if initially reluctant, member of the Guardians of the Galaxy.

Gamora's exceptional abilities are matched by her tenacious will to win. On their battle aboard Ronan's damaged warship *Dark Aster*, she withstands lethal electrocution from Nebula's electroshock staff to pull the weapon from her sister's hands.

ARMED AND DANGEROUS

A supreme assassin able to handle any scenario, Gamora can quickly master all manner of weaponry, from handheld Sakaaran Necroblasters and ship-mounted energy cannons to daggers and swords. Her preferred weapon remains her powerful sword, Godslayer.

Sakaaran Necroblaster

Ocular implants enhance vision

LIVING WEAPON

Under the harsh tutelage of Thanos, Gamora becomes a masterful warrior. Although always besting her sister, Nebula, in their brutal training sessions, Gamora was often left critically injured. Thanos rebuilt her with bionic implants to make her his ultimate weapon.

DATA FILE

> Gamora has been injected with nano-machines that have boosted her regenerative healing powers, and immune and neurological systems.

> Gamora's retractable sword, Godslayer, is so named as it can kill even an Asgardian. When faced with the monstrous energy-draining Abilisk, Gamora uses Godslayer to slice the giant beast's throat.

Metal spine and cybernetic skeletal structure

Suit made from resilient weave

Gamora's resolute focus on selling the much-desired Orb makes her initially reject the mercenary Quill's offer of a partnership. In time, she becomes one of the most loyal members of the Guardians.

Leather sword holster

Godslayer

Super-steel belt buckle

KILLER INSTINCT

Gamora's augmented physiology grants her super-human strength, agility, and stamina. These capabilities, together with her hard-won armed and unarmed combat skills and a ferocious drive to succeed, makes her invaluable to the other Guardians. Her swordplay, especially, is peerless.

Gamora's respiratory and musculoskeletal upgrades allow her to briefly outrun Nebula's M-Ship, when her enraged sister comes gunning for her on the Celestial Ego's planet.

Godslayer is Gamora's weapon of choice

Fashionable tunic tail

Lightweight reinforced wrist bands provide protection from other blades

Detachable knife used for pinpoint accurate throwing

Extendible sword with quantum-focused precision edge

GODSLAYER

Sword can be split into two blades

Hilt holds unique energy core that reduces the blade's weight

Muscle implants enhance strength and durability

Baby Groot shelters behind a determined Gamora

Gamora's strength is boosted to incredible levels through bionic augmentation. She can easily pick up and fire a huge discarded M-Ship cannon at her sister Nebula's crashed spacecraft.

FLIGHT CONTROL

A skilled pilot and navigator, Gamora is cool and capable in the most stressful situations. On the mining colony Knowhere, she takes control of a pod and outmaneuvers the faster Necrocraft fighters after her. Later, when the *Milano* is attacked by the alien Sovereign fleet she plots a successful escape route—while Quill and Rocket bicker.

Boots' springy heels provide additional cushioning

Milano navigation controls

NEBULA

Nebula is a ruthless, cybernetically enhanced assassin. A member of the Luphomoid race, she is an adopted daughter of the Mad Titan Thanos. Successive, punishing defeats at the hands of her adopted sister Gamora during childhood training sessions have led to much of Nebula's body being rebuilt with mechanical implants. Yet with every failure she grew stronger and more determined to win her father's praise—and vanquish her sister. Further teaching from Ronan the Accuser has honed her skills and also opened her eyes to the real cause of all her suffering—Thanos.

ELECTROSHOCK STAFF (LINKED)

High-friction, nanofiber blade grips

Buttons activate staff's energy charge

Linked staff is effective for close quarters combat

Headplate protects neural circuitry to augment vision and hearing

ELECTROSHOCK STAFF (SEPARATED INTO BATONS)

Tempersteel blades used against multiple attackers

Electroshock staff can discharge lethal energy bolts

Thanos places Nebula and Gamora under Ronan the Accuser's command. When Thanos asks Ronan to retrieve the valuable Orb for him, the Kree warmonger initially chooses Nebula for the mission. However, Gamora convinces Ronan that her knowledge of the planet Xandar makes her better suited to the task.

Retractable Electroshock batons

Reinforced micro-weave tunic for added protection

Fully cybernetic left arm boosts strength and conceals weapons

DAUGHTER OF THANOS

After killing a family of Luphomoids, Thanos raises the surviving child as his own, naming her Nebula. He trains her to be a killer alongside another adopted daughter, Gamora, pitting them in fierce combat with each other. Every time Gamora, Thanos' favorite, prevails, he subjects Nebula to painful machine upgrades, reminding her that she must turn her weakness into power. It is a lesson she never forgets.

Bionic musculoskeletal implants throughout Nebula's body enhance her Luphomoid physiology, granting her superhuman strength, stamina, and agility. Her unnerving appearance also gives her a psychological advantage.

AIDING THE GUARDIANS

Nebula becomes a fugitive with a bounty on her head for her part in Ronan's failed bid to destroy Xandar. Arrested by the Sovereign race, she is turned over to the Guardians as their reward for dispatching an interdimensional beast that had been tormenting the Sovereign. As the Guardians' prisoner, Nebula is reluctantly drawn into their raging battle with the power-crazed Celestial being Ego. Yet fighting side by side with the Guardians to save the universe, she discovers that her bond with Gamora is stronger than her resentment at always losing to her sister.

Metallic faceplate replicates Luphomoid blue and purple hues

Replacement mechanical hand from Ravagers' trophy box

Left arm houses contact whiplash and concussive blaster

Streamlined belt grants more freedom of movement

Suit made from fiber-reinforced hydrogel fabric for durability and adaptability

Shock-absorbing knee pads

Taken on board the *Milano* en route to Xandar, Nebula vows to kill Gamora when she gets free. However, the ship is suddenly attacked by the Sovereign's Omnicraft in pursuit of valuable batteries stolen by Rocket.

Concealed retractable tempersteel claws

CYBERNETIC IMPLANTS

Nebula's extensive bionic enhancements are wired to an internal power source. These implants enable her to heal rapidly and reshape her body when it suffers substantial damage.

Advanced prosthetics provide strength and flexibility

After their close escape from the Sovereign, the *Milano* crash-lands on the planet Berhert. While the Guardians bicker, Nebula spies that another ship has followed them through the jump point. As the craft descends, she urges her captors to free her so she can help them fight the new threat.

In the final cataclysmic battle with Ego, Nebula uses her augmented abilities to rescue Gamora when she is hurled from their rocky perch. She redeems herself in her sister's eyes and also forces Gamora to face some harsh truths about her own treatment of Nebula.

DRAX THE DESTROYER

A fierce warrior, Drax the Destroyer is a powerful and lethal combatant, brave to the point of recklessness. He tirelessly seeks and eventually finds retribution for the death of his wife Ovette and daughter Camaria at the hands of Ronan the Accuser. Never more at home than fighting alongside his valiant comrades, Drax steadfastly defends the new family he has found among the Guardians of the Galaxy.

Having rampaged across the galaxy slaying dozens of Ronan's minions in search of their master, Drax becomes known as "The Destroyer." When Nova Corps finally capture him, they incarcerate him in the high-security jail the Kyln.

Highly resilient skin, with accelerated healing factor

Drax is initially antagonistic towards Gamora, seeing her only as a means to confront her former master, Ronan. He is uninterested in the money his allies will get for the precious Orb; he simply wants to exact revenge for his family's murder.

Combat-worn holster belt and harness

Tempered metal alloy

Clip point blade for swifter, deeper cuts

Tribal markings

Ornate crossguard

Gladiatorial-styled outfit with ornamental buckles

Hard-wearing, malleable pants and padded boots

Paired blades used as first and often last line of attack

Boot scabbards for daggers

Ridged, coarse surface enhances grip

DRAX'S DAGGERS

While Drax is proficient in the use of an array of weaponry, including swords and energy blasters, his most trusted weapons are his paired knives. Forged on his homeworld to suit his close-combat style of fighting, the daggers are perfectly balanced and molded for his grip. As such, Drax keeps them razor sharp and battle-ready.

FIGHTING INSTINCTS

Born to a proud warrior people, Drax is a battle-hardened and formidable fighter. He is superhumanly strong, fast, and agile, possesses impact-resistant skin and accelerated healing abilities, and wields his dual tribal blades with ferocious skill. Brutal and unrelenting in berserker mode, he can overwhelm multiple foes at once, including several Kyln guards and a squad of alien Sakaaran soldiers. Although he is defeated by Ronan's superior power, Drax kills one of the Kree fanatic's best lieutenants, Korath the Pursuer.

Courageous, if a little foolhardy, Drax rushes into the fray with little thought for his own or sometimes his allies' safety. When the monstrous Abilisk comes for the Sovereign race's Anulax batteries, Drax jumps into the giant beast's mouth to attack it from the inside.

Drax's self-belief is boundless. He contacts Ronan to fight him one-on-one and later leaps into space to destroy a Sovereign ship while being towed by a damaged *Milano*.

SENSITIVE SOUL

Despite his notoriety as a merciless killer, Drax's motives are sincere and honorable. He will do whatever is necessary to protect or avenge his family and friends. Like the rest of his race, he is completely literal and unfamiliar with metaphors, saying exactly what he thinks and feels. Drax is drawn to the empath Mantis, whose innocence reminds him of his daughter.

Mantis can sense Drax's grief through touch

Slumped posture indicates sadness

DATA FILE

> Belying his menacing appearance and reputation as a fearsome warrior, Drax is extremely naive. He is filled with childlike wonder at the strange beauty of Ego's planet.

> Drax's perception of others is highly subjective. He genuinely believed that the blue-skinned Yondu was Peter Quill's father, claiming that they looked identical.

SAVAGE SYMBOLS

Drax's body is branded with elaborate, ritualistic scars that relate significant events from his life and his people's culture. From initiation trials to illustrious victories, these ornamental sigils are an indelible reminder of who he is and where he came from.

Vice-like grip on his deadly daggers

Tribal scars detail Drax's life story and intimidate opponents

ROCKET

Rocket is a smart-mouthed, gun-toting creature from the planet Halfworld, in the Keystone Quadrant star system. Once a wild animal known as subject "89P13," he was subjected to genetic and cybernetic upgrades to his brain and skeletal structure. These gave him an intellect as razor-sharp as his teeth, the ability to speak, enhanced strength, agility, and durability, and a snarky disposition. Initially turning his talents toward a criminal career, in league with his best friend Groot, the two mercenaries become unlikely heroes after they help form the Guardians of the Galaxy.

Teeth can bite through metal

Quadruple barrels

Configured for ion pulse stun mode

BOUNTY HUNTER

Before joining the Guardians, Rocket and Groot often work as bounty hunters. They try netting a 40,000-unit bounty by capturing Peter Quill for the Ravager Yondu, but the failed attempt gets them sent to the Kyln prison. Here, Rocket is held for 13 counts of theft, seven of mercenary activity, 15 of arson, and public drunkenness. After joining the Guardians to save the planet Xandar from the Kree terrorist Ronan the Accuser, Rocket's and Groot's criminal records, and those of their new teammates, are expunged.

Rocket has escaped from prison 23 times, including his escape from the interstellar prison known as the Kyln, alongside the Guardians.

TRE-VA5 detachable heat scope

Cushioned elbow rest adapter

Dual internal RE-1FF laser/ion power cells

Forward sight with weighted auto leveler

ROCKET'S LASER CANNON

Handle bar and ion pulse secondary trigger

Protective hood extender

FLYING MAMMAL

Cybernetically engineered to pilot any spacecraft, Rocket's enhanced reflexes probably make him better at flying the Guardians' ship, the *Milano*, than Peter Quill, though Quill would never admit it. Rocket is also a master inventor, engineer, and weapons expert. From high-powered cannons and planet-leveling explosives to jetpacks and nanobot welders, he can create or fix most devices.

Rocket's nimble hand operates ship via joystick

Rocket thinks he is the mastermind behind the Guardians, but his schemes don't always go to plan. He devises their escape from the Kyln prison and much of the attacks on the Kree terrorist Ronan and the Celestial Ego.

Sensitive ears
with acute
hearing

Outfit stolen from
a spaceport
shopping plaza

Vest secretly
treated to repel
space fleas

"Katie"
BN1 blaster

"Vicki"
BA-17 ion pistol,
taken from
fallen Ravager

Dexterous clawed
paws adept at
climbing

Rocket invents "aero-rigs" for the Guardians. The devices are worn like backpacks and allow the team to fly during close combat. Drax doesn't like to wear his, though, as he claims the straps hurt his sensitive nipples.

GROUCHY GUARDIAN

Rocket has very sensitive feelings. He is easily offended when he thinks the other Guardians look down on him. When people call him names like "rodent" or "vermin" or even "trash panda" it makes him furious and he overreacts—he even bites. Rocket is bitter about the torturous experiments that were done to him, which can make him spiteful at times.

Rocket's enhanced senses, animal instincts, and tactical smarts come to the fore when he rigs an elaborate series of booby traps that take out a squad of Ravagers trying to collect a bounty on the Guardians.

At first they annoy each other to distraction, but when Rocket and Yondu are forced to work together to defeat Ego, they end up earning each other's respect. Rocket finally concedes that they share much in common and is deeply saddened when Yondu sacrifices himself to save Quill.

DATA FILE

> Rocket's attempts to copy humanoid facial expressions, such as sarcastic winks, often backfire badly.

> Rocket's navigation panel contains data on planets like Drez-Lar (2 moons), Hala (2 moons), and Terma (5 moons).

GROOT

Groot is a conscious, self-aware plant (*Flora colossus*) from Taluhnia. He is best friends with Rocket and they work together as mercenaries, with Rocket's brains complementing Groot's considerable brawn. After they accept a bounty on the outlaw Peter Quill, the two wind up in the Kyln prison with the rest of the future Guardians of the Galaxy. When the Guardians join forces to stop the Kree zealot Ronan the Accuser, Groot sacrifices himself to save his new friends. Thanks to Rocket, though, he regenerates.

Groot is no stranger to prison. His criminal record includes three counts of grievous bodily harm, 15 counts of escape from incarceration, and three counts of mercenary activity. His known criminal associates include Rocket and Tibius Lark.

Groot can be rather violent, for a plant. Most of the time he is sedate and gentle, but when the occasion demands, Groot enjoys teaming up with Rocket for a bit of savage destruction.

"I AM GROOT"

According to Rocket, Groot's vocabulary is limited to "I" and "am" and "Groot," exclusively in that order. The only recent exception is when he affectionately declares "We are Groot" to the Guardians. Groot conveys a lot of information with intonation, cadence, and body language. Rocket reads him well, filling in gaps where necessary. The rest of the Guardians slowly begin to understand Groot, too.

JOINING THE GUARDIANS

Kyln prison guards try to put pants on Groot, but he just rips them off. Groot doesn't like clothes, or conforming to societal norms. That makes him a great fit for Peter Quill's gang of outcasts. When Rocket explains that they need to team up with the others to escape, Groot is happy to oblige, but he kicks off Rocket's plan before anyone else is ready.

Eyes are the only visibly non-woody part of Groot's body

Moss grows on shoulder and chest plates

Arms grow back when severed

Hands can rapidly extend for aggressive purposes

Limbs are a fusing of twisted vines

Baby Groot is mistreated when he and Rocket are caught by mutinous Ravagers. They taunt him, poke at him, and pour drinks all over him—but Groot is most upset about the cute little Ravager mascot suit they force him to wear. Once Groot is free, he works out all his pent-up frustrations in a violent rage.

The Ravager Yondu likes Baby Groot. He sends "Twig" on a mission to retrieve something that will aid their escape from the mutineers. Unfortunately, while adult Groot was never particularly adept at following instructions, Baby Groot finds listening comprehension even more challenging.

BABY GROOT

Rocket mourns Groot when he is obliterated on Xandar. He saves a twig from Groot and plants it, from which a new Baby Groot grows. This new Groot is not quite the same as the old Groot. He is more like a clone, retaining none of the old Groot's knowledge or memories. Baby Groot enjoys music and dancing. He is boisterous and cantankerous, but still adored by the crew.

Bark smells like cedar and cinnamon

Occasionally sprouts leaves, which Groot eats

Hands snatch bugs and other snacks

Feet absorb water from puddles

Switch starts detonation sequence

Baby Groot is mesmerized by the "Death Button"

DESTROYING EGO

Keen to prove his worth, Baby Groot is the only team member small enough to carry out Rocket's plan to destroy the evil Celestial Ego. Groot's instructions are simple: plant Rocket's improvised bomb in Ego's planetary core, flip the left switch first, then the next switch, and then press the next button. At that point Groot has five minutes to escape. Rocket warns him not to press the last button or the bomb will explode immediately!

Anulax Battery

IMPROVISED BOMB

PARTNERS IN CRIME

There is no doubt that Rocket loves Groot, though his role changes from best friend to parent with Groot's regeneration. Rocket takes time to teach Baby Groot valuable life lessons and lecture him for his foul language.

RONAN THE ACCUSER

A genocidal Kree warlord, Ronan the Accuser is bent on revenge against his ancestral enemies, the Xandarians. He refuses to respect the new peace treaty with Xandar, and bargains with the Mad Titan Thanos, promising to provide him with the mysterious Orb of Morag in exchange for help destroying the planet Xandar. When Ronan recovers the Orb and discovers the power of the Infinity Stone hidden within, he betrays Thanos and attacks Xandar on his own. He is vanquished by the Guardians of the Galaxy before he can achieve his victory.

Accuser cowl covers bald head, painted with permanent black resin

Condemnation warhead

Conviction energy input adapter melds with Infinity Stone

Prior to going rogue, Ronan was one of the Kree Empire's foremost military leaders. Scornful of the peace treaty with the Xandarians, he pledges to destroy Xandar. He undergoes the Kree Ritual of War with the aid of his Exolon Monks.

Ancestral Kree battle armor is uncomfortable and smells like tar

Cosmi-Rod hammer

If Ronan wielded the Infinity Stone with his bare hands it would eventually destroy him. Harnessing its vast cosmic energies by placing it within his Cosmi-Rod hammer gives Ronan the power to wipe out all life on Xandar.

THE KREE

Ronan is a native of the planet Hala, the ancestral homeworld of the blue-skinned Kree and also a race of sentient plants known as the Cotati. Kree are superhumanly strong and immensely resilient. They can regenerate from even the most severe injuries, and live centuries or more. The Kree and Xandarians have been at war for 1,000 years, and generations of Ronan's own Imperial family have died in the conflict. He intends not only to avenge them, but also take to the opportunity to annex the domain of his erstwhile ally Thanos.

Krehalium-plated war apron

Kree "skull-crusher" weighted battle boots

DATA FILE

> While on board the *Dark Aster*, Ronan sleeps in a pit filled with Celestial blood.

> Ronan takes a blast to the chest from Rocket's Hadron Enforcer. Although the weapon has the power to destroy entire moons, Ronan is largely unscathed.

DARK ASTER

Ronan's Kree warship is the *Dark Aster*. This mighty vessel is 9,509 years old, approximately 3 miles (5 km) wide, and has 30 rotating segments on each wing. The ship itself carries no offensive weapons but acts as carrier for a fleet of 4,000 potent Necrocraft.

Fleet of Necrocraft swarm Xandar's defenses

Each wing segment can rotate independently

KORATH THE PURSUER

Ronan's most trusted ally is Korath the Pursuer. He is a genetically and cybernetically enhanced Kree operative who volunteered for an experimental Kree weapons program. Super-strong and relentless, Korath trained with two of Thanos' adopted daughters, Gamora and Nebula, enduring similar bio-tech upgrades as them. Commanding a platoon of Sakaaran soldiers, Korath is sent to retrieve the Orb from the planet Morag, but is outwitted by Star-Lord. Later, Korath warns his master that he is making a mistake by defying Thanos. He falls in a brutal duel with the Guardian Drax while defending the *Dark Aster*.

In addition to Korath, Ronan's retinue also includes Thanos' adopted daughters, Nebula and Gamora. Gamora betrays Ronan to obtain the Orb for herself. Nebula remains in the Kree's service, but only because it provides an opportunity to strike against her hated father.

Bone-like helmet faceplate can be removed to expose mouthparts

Fires quantum energy bolts that rip molecules apart

Crystalline power cell compartment

SAKAARANS

Several races originated on the junk planet Sakaar. The insectoid humanoids known simply as "Sakaarans" resented the local Scrappers disturbing their hives and emigrated off-world. The four-fingered soldier cast are hermaphrodites, and are born in hives maintained by queens.

KORATH'S N20-75 DISRUPTER RIFLE

Trigger lock calibrated to Kree body temperature

Armies of Sakaaran mercenaries are commonly employed by the Kree. Their loyalty is easily bought with an ample supply of carcasses for feeding on and laying their eggs in. Their weaponry and armor is bioengineered—the latter fuses to their exoskeleton.

Necroblaster rifle powered by slimy endoplasm

THE KYLN

The Kyln is a remote, high-security penal facility run by the Nova Corps, the intergalactic military and police force of the Nova Empire. Notorious for the cruelty and corruption of its guards, the deep-space prison holds some of the deadliest criminals in the galaxy. Peter Quill, Gamora, Rocket, and Groot are transported to the Kyln after being arrested for disorder and affray on Xandar, the capital of the Nova Empire.

Incarcerated with some of the worst felons in the galaxy, Peter Quill comes under the protection of Rocket and Groot. The duo still intend to collect a bounty for handing him over to Yondu—after they escape from the Kyln.

PRISONER BINDERS

Energy cuffs paralyze inmates who try to escape

As a former accomplice of Ronan the Accuser, who has slaughtered many of the Kyln inmates' families, Gamora becomes a target of their hostility. They come close to killing her when the feared prisoner Drax intervenes, keen to settle his own score with Gamora.

Central communications tower

Administration area and hospital

Main prison cell block

MAXIMUM SECURITY

Floating in the farthest reaches of the galaxy, the Kyln was constructed by Nova Corps as the ultimate prison. The high-tech, city-sized penitentiary is extensively fortified and staffed by aggressive, heavily armed guards and deadly drones. However, when the Kree warlord Ronan the Accuser comes in search of a mysterious and valuable Orb, his forces "cleanse" the facility, eliminating everyone on board.

Dense, compacted base provides ballast

Primary forward-thrust engine

PRISONER WEAPONS

To defend themselves from violent fellow inmates or equally brutal guards, Kyln's prisoners create all manner of improvised weaponry. Some double as tools that could be used in a bid to escape.

Rags used for handgrip

Metal pipe ground into a jagged blade

IMPROVISED SHANK

HOMEMADE GRAPPLE

Cooking stand bent into sturdy hooks

In response to serious escape attempts, the Kyln can call on a quick reaction force who wield high-powered energy cannons. These military-grade weapons are deployed as a last resort to subdue desperate and uncooperative prisoners.

DATA FILE

> The Kyln guards wear security bands hard-wired into their nervous systems. These devices give them access to all areas of the prison.

> While on the run in Knowhere, Quill uses a mining pod's powerful clamps to tear into one of Ronan's Necrocraft, and take control of the starship and its weaponry.

INMATE'S PROSTHETIC LEG

Prosthetic leg cost Peter Quill 30,000 units

Rotor knee joint provides flexibility

Hydraulic piston acts as a shock absorber

Kyln's inmates are assigned yellow jumpsuits

Each stripe's color represents a crime, from burglary to murder

BREAKING OUT

Having boasted of escaping from 22 prisons, Rocket devises an elaborate scheme to break out of the Kyln. It requires a guard's security wristband to access and take over the central watchtower, an inmate's prosthetic leg, and disabling a Quarnyx Battery in order to trigger the prison's emergency lockdown. While events don't go to plan, Rocket and his motley group manage to escape and form an uneasy alliance.

KNOWHERE

Knowhere is a mining outpost built inside the severed head of an ancient Celestial being. It is a lawless place that attracts criminals keen to mine rare Celestial bodyparts, which are highly prized in black markets across the galaxy. It is also home to the infamous Collector, Taneleer Tivan, who has agreed to pay Gamora four billion units to procure the precious Orb for his museum.

Star-Lord's ship, the Milano, approaches Knowhere

Pod hulls built with near-indestructible, industrial-grade materials

Knowhere boasts the galaxy's largest collection of flora, fauna, and relics

Ronan arrives in Knowhere after receiving a transmission from Drax challenging him to a fight. Ronan easily overpowers Drax, and with Nebula's help, retrieves the Orb from Star-Lord.

Mounting points for various tools including claws and harpoons

MINING POD

SOVEREIGN

The Sovereign are a race of gold-skinned people with a huge superiority complex. These beings are pompous and arrogant, but many in the galaxy consider them airheads. Dealings with the Sovereign can be perilous. They are easily insulted and transgressions against them usually result in swift and harsh punishments. The Sovereign fear being seen as weak, and so resort to summary executions rather than allowing word to reach their neighbors of their profound incompetence. They are led by the High Priestess Ayesha, who makes a deal with the Guardians of the Galaxy that both parties come to deeply regret.

The Sovereign homeworld (coordinates: M49 5IOL339P21+H9LNI31) is a conglomeration of planets and moons held together by a miracle of engineering. The configuration is a blend of art and science, pulling an entire solar system into a single clump.

Crown fused to throne, as authority is bound to office

Naturally golden skin

The Abilisk is an inter-dimensional beast with a taste for the Sovereign's Anulax Batteries. The Guardians are hired to kill the tough-skinned creature, but its muscular tentacles, gaping maw, and periodic blasts of quantum splatter make this a formidable task.

Symbolic protection of the people's voice

Intricately detailed bodice

AYESHA

The beautiful and arrogant Ayesha is the High Priestess of the Sovereign. She is their figurehead, but still answerable to the governing council. At 6 ft 7 in (2 m) tall, Ayesha towers above the Guardians, and even her own Sovereign attendants. Like all Sovereign, she is vain and self-centered—she isn't actually concerned about the Anulax Batteries stolen by the Guardians, she is far more angry about being humiliated.

After defeating the Abilisk, Rocket decides to steal Anulax Batteries himself, which sets in motion a series of cascading misadventures. His lack of respect causes the Sovereign to tirelessly hunt the Guardians across the galaxy.

Unadorned hands for unhindered executions

SOVEREIGN FLEET

The Sovereign fleet is comprised of thousands of Omnicraft. Since they are unmanned drones, distance to a target is no obstacle. Omnicraft can be flown on autopilot while their operators do something more entertaining. Despite the lack of any personal risk, the Sovereign try to avoid battles with other worlds that they cannot win.

Pilot projection screen

AYESHA'S OMNICRAFT FIGHTER

The Sovereign would never dream of dirtying their hands in combat, let alone risking their own lives on the battlefront. Pilots remotely drive their Omnicraft using flight simulators installed at the Sovereign Mission Control Center.

Stabilizer wings and propulsion field

The Sovereign Mission Control Center is a theater of buzzing remote pods, lined in tiered rows. The inept Fleet Admiral observes them from above, at times joined by the anxious High Priestess.

Laser cannon

Camera, scanners, and data relay

Indicator light changes with maturations

DATA FILE

> Ayesha has four handmaidens who attend to her every need.

> When Ayesha travels to other planets, her attendants lay a blue carpet for her to walk on, thereby preventing Ayesha from sullying her feet with impure alien dirt.

Pod for germination, ripening, birthing, and metamorphosis

ADAM'S BIRTHING POD

The Sovereign reproduce artificially in birthing pods. Offspring are genetically engineered by the community to be flawless (according to Sovereign standards, anyway), and designed for both physical and mental perfection. Adam is Ayesha's ultimate creation—the next step in Sovereign evolution. His predetermined purpose is to destroy the Guardians of the Galaxy.

Nutrient cables

EGO

Ego is a Celestial—a being who possesses god-like powers and supreme arrogance. Coming into existence as a disembodied entity, Ego creates a planet around his consciousness to protect himself, and sends corporeal avatars into the cosmos to learn about other life forms. Discovering that all life is disappointingly temporary, he finally finds his purpose—to destroy and renew the universe as an extension of himself. To realize this "Expansion," however, he needs the power of another Celestial, which he finds in his long-lost son, Peter Quill.

Collar and robe bestow a noble, heroic bearing

Wise expression assumed to gain trust

Ego returns to Earth to be with Meredith Quill three times, coming to love her as his "river lily." In time, though, he realizes her love is causing him to drift from his plan and reluctantly implants a brain tumor in Meredith, which leads to her death.

FATHER OF QUILL

To prepare for the Expansion, Ego seeds countless planets with a fragment of himself. He also sires children on these planets whom he hopes will inherit his Celestial gene—with no success. On Earth he meets and falls in love with Meredith Quill, with whom he has a son, Peter. Decades later, when Ego hears of an Earth man who has held an Infinity Stone without dying, he realizes he has found his true heir, one who will help him power his Expansion.

Ornately detailed cuffs reinforce Ego's majestic appearance

On the planet Berhert, Ego's affable personality and paternal banter succeed in allaying Peter's suspicions. He asks him, Gamora, and Drax to accompany him to his own world where he will reveal Peter's very special heritage.

DATA FILE

> Ego's humanoid avatar has a digestive system, pain receptors, and most human attributes, yet can also withstand exposure to space. However, his fragile avatar must return to his world regularly to rejuvenate.

> The energy of Ego's world can be tapped by his son, Peter, and even make him immortal as long as the light burns within the planet.

Highest-quality knee-length boots complete Ego's elaborate illusion

Ego's planet is a testament to the Celestial's taste and vanity. It is a sun-drenched wonderland teeming with beautiful alien plant life, multicolored self-forming baubles, and bejeweled structures. It also harbors a dark secret.

Ego's true nature is revealed after Peter blasts him

Human physiology can remake itself while in contact with the planet

Every atom of Ego is linked to the "Light"

Beneath the surface of Ego's planet lie the skeletal remains of Ego's other children. He killed them as none possessed the Celestial gene necessary for his Expansion.

Suit is remade along with the rest of the body

CELESTIAL POWERS

Ego is a Celestial, a race of primordial, cosmic entities who existed long before the Asgardians or Dark Elves. These all-powerful beings were revered yet feared by many in the universe for their ruthless use of the Infinity Stones. As a Celestial, Ego can manipulate matter and energy, creating objects and living beings at will. In his purest form, he is ethereal and eternal, but when required creates physical avatars to travel the cosmos.

When Peter discovers Ego's real plan and what he did to his mother, he fires on him. In retaliation, an enraged Ego strikes his son with an energy spike to siphon his Celestial power. If Peter won't willingly join him, then he will become a living battery for Ego's Expansion.

LIVING PLANET

Outside the edge of the known universe lies Ego's planet, a world no larger than Earth's moon. After flickering into life, Ego learns how to control matter and creates a planetary shell to protect his essence: his "Light." Ego can manipulate all aspects of his planet, even manifesting his consciousness as an immense face across its surface.

Deep within the planet is a vast neural network that connects Ego's mind to every part of his world. It enables him to trap the Guardians when they attempt to blow up his planet.

MANTIS

An orphaned larva found by Ego on an unidentified world, Mantis is raised by the Celestial on his planet. She possesses powerful empathic abilities that enable her to feel and alter the emotions of others. Mantis submissively uses her powers to assist her benefactor in realizing his Expansion plans. Upon meeting the Guardians, she forms a quick friendship with her fellow misfits, and helps them defeat Ego when he reveals his real and terrifying nature.

Growing up alone on Ego's planet, Mantis knows little of her origins and lacks simple social skills. She poorly mimics the gestures of others in an attempt to fit in.

Antennae glow when Mantis uses her empathic powers

Petal-like, openwork leather design trails up arms

Mantis has been by Ego's side for as long as she can remember. Assisting him to locate his "children," she eventually discovers the horrific fate of those who do not possess the Celestial gene. With nowhere else to turn, she is trapped in lonely servitude to Ego—until the Guardians arrive.

Green-and-black outfit resembles Mantis' Terran insect namesake

Raised in isolation, Mantis has no experience of raw emotions. When the Guardian Drax asks her to sense his feelings, his unbridled mirth at Quill's embarrassment overwhelms her with delight.

TRUE FEELINGS

A formidable empath, Mantis can sense and modify the feelings of others simply by touching them. Her abilities are invaluable to Ego, enabling him to sleep on his galaxy-spanning search for a true Celestial heir. She also shows great mental and physical resilience when she helps the Guardians take on her malevolent mentor.

Winglike coat tails

EMOTIONAL MANIPULATION

A true innocent unaware of much beyond Ego and his all-consuming mission, Mantis is highly curious about the Guardians. She uses her powers on Quill, revealing his romantic feelings towards Gamora, much to his discomfort, and explains that she can also manipulate emotions.

Happy expression upon sensing Quill's love for Gamora

Mantis' mere touch lays Quill's emotions bare

Ruched leggings

Ribbed ankle-length boots

Mantis is no more than a pet to Ego. Despite her importance on his journeys into space, the Celestial barely acknowledges her presence when he displays his story to the Guardians. As the only surviving being on Ego's planet, Mantis knows how capricious and dangerous her master can be and accepts her place as his "useful flea."

Virtual 3D model of Ego's planet

Thought-controlled diorama display

MODEL OF EGO'S WORLD

After spending time with the Guardians, Mantis discovers a rare, contrary, and potent emotion—love. Sharing Drax's great sadness at the memory of his daughter makes her care for him and the Guardians.

DATA FILE

> Mantis has lived in fear of Ego for so long that when she is finally free of him she experiences her first real sense of wonder at the Ravagers' funeral for Yondu.

> Mantis' body is very resilient. When she is struck in the head by a large, jagged piece of starship debris, she is knocked out but otherwise unharmed.

A NEW GUARDIAN

Mantis demonstrates great bravery helping her newfound allies battle Ego when he unleashes the full force of his planet against them. With encouragement from Drax, she summons all her strength to put the enraged Celestial to sleep, buying the Guardians time to put their plan into action.

Yondu

Nebula

Star-Lord

Rocket

Drax

Mantis

Gamora

Index

Main entries are shown in **bold**.

Star emblem
emblazoned
on chest

Carbon polymer
material withstands
knives and bullets

Leather strap holds
armor in place over
Cap's upper arm

Patriotic red-
white-and-blue
color scheme

CAPTAIN AMERICA'S WORLD WAR II COMBAT UNIFORM

ACKNOWLEDGMENTS

DK would like to thank Kevin Feige, Louis D'Esposito, Victoria Alonso, Stephen Broussard, Eric Carroll, Craig Kyle, Jeremy Latcham, Nate Moore, Jonathan Schwartz, Trinh Tran, Brad Winderbaum, Brian Chapek, Mary Livanos, Zoie Nagelhout, Kevin Wright, Michelle Momplaisir, Richie Palmer, Mitch Bell, David Grant, Dave Bushore, Sarah Beers, Will Corona Pilgrim, Corinna Vistan, Ariel Gonzalez, Adam Davis, Eleena Khamedoost, Cameron Ramsay, Kyle Quigley, Michele Blood, Jacqueline Ryan, David Galluzzi, Ryan Potter, Erika Denton, Jeff Willis, Randy McGowan, Bryan Parker, Percival Lanuza, Vince Garcia, Matt Delmanowski, Alex Scharf, Jim Velasco, and Andrew Starbin at Marvel Studios; Nick Fratto, Caitlin O'Connell, and Jeff Youngquist at Marvel; and Chelsea Alon, Elana Cohen, Stephanie Everett, Kurt Hartman, and Julia Vargas at Disney. DK would also like to thank Vanessa Bird for proofreading and the index, and Natalie Edwards for editorial assistance.

PICTURE CREDITS
Page 10 (middle left): Flagg, James Montgomery, Artist. *I want you for U.S. Army: nearest recruiting station / James Montgomery Flagg.* United States, ca. 1917. Photograph. Retrieved from the Library of Congress, https://www.loc.gov/item/96507165/. (Accessed January 10, 2018.)

AVAILABLE NOW ON VARIOUS FORMATS INCLUDING DIGITAL WHERE APPLICABLE FOR THE FOLLOWING FILMS:
Iron Man, The Incredible Hulk, Iron Man 2, Thor, Captain America: The First Avenger, Marvel's The Avengers, Iron Man 3, Thor: The Dark World, Captain America: The Winter Soldier, Guardians of the Galaxy, Avengers: Age of Ultron, Ant-Man, Captain America: Civil War, Doctor Strange, Guardians of the Galaxy Vol. 2, Thor: Ragnarok, Black Panther, Marvel Studios' Avengers: Infinity War, Ant-Man And The Wasp
© 2018 MARVEL

Senior Editor David Fentiman
Senior Designer Robert Perry
Project Editor Ruth Amos
Editors Kathryn Hill, Matt Jones, and Cefn Ridout
Designers Nick Avery, Jon Hall, Gary Hyde, Ian Midson, and Simon Murrell
Pre-Production Producer Siu Yin Chan
Producer Zara Markland
Managing Editor Sadie Smith
Managing Art Editor Vicky Short
Publisher Julie Ferris
Art Director Lisa Lanzarini
Publishing Director Simon Beecroft

Additional text by Ruth Amos, David Fentiman, Matt Jones, and Cefn Ridout

Additional reprographic assistance from Steve Crozier, Chris Gould, Jon Hall, Sunil Sharma, Anne Sharples, and Jessica Tapolcai
Cover reprographics by Tom Morse

First American Edition, 2018
Published in the United States by DK Publishing
345 Hudson Street, New York, New York 10014

DK, a Division of Penguin Random House LLC
18 19 20 21 22 10 9 8 7 6 5 4 3 2 1
001–310806–September/2018

DK books are available at special discounts when purchased in bulk for sales promotions, premiums, fund-raising, or educational use. For details, contact: DK Publishing Special Markets, 345 Hudson Street, New York, New York 10014
SpecialSales@dk.com

Printed and bound in China

A WORLD OF IDEAS:
SEE ALL THERE IS TO KNOW

www.dk.com